From Minutes that matter to Sermons that Surprise

From Minutes that matter to Sermons that Surprise

52 Homilies for Preachers, with Bonus Section

Mario Weyers

CWI
Christian World Imprints

First Published in 2019 by

Christian World Imprints
Christian Publishing & Books from India
H-12 Bali Nagar, **New Delhi-110015**
info@christianworldimprints.com
www.ChristianWorldImprints.com
Phone: +91 11 25465925

ISBN: 978-93-5148-314-4

Cataloging in Publication Data--DK

Courtesy: D.K. Agencies (P) Ltd. <docinfo@dkagencies.com>

Weyers, Mario, 1973- **author.**
From minutes that matter to sermons that surprise : 52 homilies for preachers, with bonus section / Mario Weyers.
pages cm
ISBN 9789351483144

1. Sermons, English. 2. Pastoral care--Sermons. I. Title.

LCC BV4253.W49 2019 | DDC 252 23

Printed in India.

Contents

SERMONS FOR FIXING WHAT IS BROKEN: PREACHING AS PROPHETIC RESPONSIBILITY

INTRODUCTION

Thank you for choosing to read this book! I only write on what I believe and feel passionate about and hope that you, in reading this content, will be inspired as well. I do hope that the content will do one of two things or both. One outcome, I sincerely wish for, is for you to become a lifelong student of the Bible and the other that fits well with the first is that you will share its contents with others.

If it so happens that you find yourself in ministry that should come quite naturally. If you are not, I pray that it will not keep you from sharing your surprise finds in the Word of God with your associates and specific network of people.

I do not wish to disappoint you, but should you be searching for the different genres of preaching or how to become a great orator or preacher then this read is not what you would like to spend your time on. This book is to motivate and confirm that preaching still matters especially in a post-Christendom context and the time spend preparing for doing that does indeed count for a lot.

Knowledge of Christianity and Christ's saving mediation is rather limited among post-Christian communities which do not have a historic bond with the Christendom era. Post-Christian seekers and those interested in what Christianity teaches need to hear the Gospel and its wider content numerous times. Why? Because Christian culture seems strange to the current and upcoming generation who is not that familiar with the content of the Bible, the Gospel narrative or Christian culture as practised inside the context of a congregation. Teaching the content of the Bible, preaching to those who are eager to listen and releasing Biblical principles is what I believe will become even more so the primary work of the Church in a post-Christendom culture as communities become more secularised and individuals life's more fragmented.

In the past, Western culture was influenced and shaped by an overall biblical worldview. With the rise of science, technology and new philosophies the church started competing with other voices and many of these voices were mostly in direct opposition to what the Church through the ages proclaimed and preached. Today, these other voices seems to be the dominant one as dissonance between faith and reason are on the increase.

The first section of this book is therefore to encourage those in the ministry of preaching and teaching to be disciplined in not neglecting this important call and service to God and his people. The time spent in prayer, reading and researching are indeed minutes that seriously matters in bringing God's living Word to the community. Also to encourage those in carrying this responsibility of preaching and teaching, to allow the Holy Spirit to keep on surprising you in unexpected ways in revealing the powerful truth in the Bible. It is only when we allow and trust God to surprise us from within His word that we are geared to release an authentic revelation or word to those that desperately need it.

The second part of the book consists of my sermons, arranged according to the English alphabet and divided into two categories: sermons for *Feeding* and sermons for *Fixing*, which is proof that God has indeed surprised me in preparing sermons over a span of 21 years. Choosing these sermons for this publication were indeed no easy task. But in order to be true to the topic of this publication and myself I chose those sermons that was not only created by my education, own reading or understanding, but from within the silent whisper of the Holy Spirit who was promised to guide us in all truth.

Under the heading: *Sermons for Feeding* 26 messages are there. Under the heading: *Sermons for Fixing* another 26 teachings follow to bring the total of sermon messages to 52 – a message for you to use, share or expand on per Sunday or midweek meeting.

Two main criteria that will surface, as you study the second half of the book, are two principles that are well respected in Reformed Theology when preparing for teaching and preaching:

- *Scripture is to be interpreted in light of Scripture – comparing Scripture with Scripture.*
- *The Christological principle – which states that Scripture is to be interpreted in light of God's central revelation in Jesus Christ.*

I would like to elaborate on both these key principles in relating to - and releasing the word of God in preaching and teaching.

In regard to the first principle, I want to include not only the importance of comparing Old Testament Scripture with Old Testament Scripture or New Testament Scripture with New Testament Scripture, but inter-relating the Old and New in interpreting God's word for today. This is particularly important when preparing sermons and preaching to postmodern communities who, from lack of understanding, consider Scripture to be fragmented, inconsistent and at its worse a paradox.

When preaching sermons that do relate to both the Old and New Testaments (as in the New Testament confirming or elaborating on Scripture in the Old Testament or The Old Testament being brought to completion in the New Testament) one not only promotes the unity and inter-connectedness of Scripture, but targets the general misconception that the Bible contradicts itself. For many postmodern individuals it can be surprising to find that the Bible is mostly holistic in its presentation of the Gospel and to be more precise that the Old Testament are brought to light only when reading it through the scope of the New. Understanding that the Old and New Testaments are closely connected and revealing that in our preaching, is what I believe brings the word of God to life.

The *Christological principle* for me is an evangelical one. You can simply not preach on the person or character of Christ and the realisation of His kingdom without elaborating on Jesus role as the anointed One who was sent to die for the sins of the world. Preaching on Christ is nothing less than the inherent message of Good news, for Christ and the cross are inseparable. Preaching on Christ is by implication the intrinsic proclamation of the gospel, for Jesus is the central revelation of God's love. Romans 1:16 states:

"For I am not ashamed of the gospel, because it is the power of God that brings salvation to everyone who believes: first to the Jew, then to the Gentile."[1]

May we not consider preaching to be important in producing growing numbers or gratitude towards us in our churches, but to make Jesus Christ the main act on centre stage with the Old and New Testaments as powerful stage lights clearly alighting the birth, ministry, death and resurrection of Jesus Christ.

Mario Weyers
New Zealand (2018).

[1] All scriptures are quoted from the NIV – New International Version.

THE ROLE OF THE LOCAL PASTOR

THE ROLE OF THE PASTOR DURING THE AGES:[2]

In preindustrial times, before the Industrial revolution, societies where mainly small, rural, depended largely on local resources and had only a few specialized occupations of which clergy was one. In such a limited context was the local minister labelled as a general leader in the community (apart from shepherding the congregation), because of the fact that the pastor was, among only a few occupations then, a professionally trained employee of the Church. In general the minister would serve on the school board as well as the district council. He was respected for his general contribution to the welfare of society. Therefore, clergy was heavily labelled as *community leaders.*

In the eighteenth century, Europe experienced a dramatic rise in technological invention known as the Industrial Revolution. Work that in the past was depended on largely person-or animals was now done by machines and in less time. One of the outcomes of the Industrial revolution was the rise of urban centres which was responsible for workers flocking to factories for jobs and better incomes:

---

[2] Dr. Jack Barentsen: lecture on Models of Pastoral Leadership at the Evangelical Theological Faculty in Leuven, Belgium in February 2013.

The new generation became less preoccupied with maintaining family land and traditions and more focused on acquiring wealth and achieving upward mobility for themselves. People wanted their children and their children's children to continue to rise to the top. Life was changing quickly and the long- (healthy) established traditions of agricultural eras did not apply to life in the cities. Masses of people were moving to new environments and often found themselves faced with horrendous conditions of filth, overcrowding and poverty. Eventually concerns over the exploitation of workers led to the formation of labour unions and laws.[3]

It was in such a challenging environment that many from an agricultural background could not maintain their emotional and spiritual wellbeing and needed clergy to function from a mostly caregiving role and one that was recognised as the *Shepherd model.* In due time the role of the minister as a pastoral caregiver was established as a profession in the caregiving industry where the minister was mainly responsible for the wellbeing of his flock.

After the occurrence of the First –and Second World Wars we find once again a shift in the role of the parish minister or local pastor. People in general were devastated by two world wars that badly reflected on how cruel and selfish the nature of mankind is. Spiritual leadership was needed that would guide and direct congregations and communities to keep to the so-called: straight and narrow. The role of the pastor now took on the label of a *director of an organization* that mainly had to steer his people, which God had entrusted to him or her, in the Godly and humane direction.

THE ROLE OF THE PASTOR IN A POSTINDUSTRIAL SOCIETY:

With the turn of the century we find ourselves in what is known as the *information* or *digital society.* Unlike industrial societies that are rooted in the production of material goods, information societies are based on the production of information services. Since, the economy of information societies is driven by knowledge, power lies with

[3] Introduction to Sociology, Rice University-Houston Texas, 2017.

those in charge of storing and distributing information. Individuals in a post-industrial society are likely to be employed as sellers of services. *Service providers* as they are commonly known. It is in such a context that ministers find themselves as *life coaches or spiritual experts* that "sell" information and services to member clients on how to successfully advance through the different phases of life. Member clients are less interested in theology, dogma or high church debates than they are in *how to deal with…* or *how to cope with…*matters of life in a severely complicated and fragmented society.

Preaching that does not fit the *feeding* or *fixing* category will not provide the service expectation of Post-Christendom society. The leadership ability of the local pastor may graciously be respected or at the most tolerated, but if clergy do not deliver information that can service the fragmented and high paced life of postmodern society their relevance in preaching and teaching will be reflected in the numbers on any given Sunday.

In our secularised and highly individualised environment preaching and teaching are unfortunately not valued for its academic or philosophical contribution to society than it is for fast and effective selling of information and solutions.[4]

[4] The sermons presented in this book is constructed to apply to the criteria mentioned here. It is mainly practical, condensed and focused on teaching what is core and essential to the topic at hand. It is more structured on application and less on explanation.

WHY PREACHING AND TEACHING MATTERS?

Preaching and teaching matters for two very important reasons. People, whether in groups or as individuals, need to be *fed* and secondly there are always situations that need *fixing* in our communities. I believe that for these tasks God has entrusted two kinds of *boxes* to those of us that are in ministry. The first is what I like to refer to as the *Lunch Box. This is a symbol of feeding – by means of our weekly preaching of the Word- those that are subject to our ministry. The other is a Tool box. Which is a reminder that society are in constant need of fixing and therefore do need the instruction and teaching ministry of the Church.*

FEEDING THE HUNGRY:[5]

15 When they had finished eating, Jesus said to Simon Peter, "Simon son of John, do you love me more than these?"

"Yes, Lord," he said, "you know that I love you."

Jesus said, "Feed my lambs."

16 Again Jesus said, "Simon son of John, do you love me?"

He answered, "Yes, Lord, you know that I love you."

---

[5] *John 21:15-17 New International Version (NIV)*

Jesus said, "Take care of my sheep."

17 *The third time he said to him, "Simon son of John, do you love me?"*

Peter was hurt because Jesus asked him the third time, "Do you love me?" He said, "Lord, you know all things; you know that I love you."

Jesus said, "Feed my sheep."

Peter has denied Jesus three times, now Jesus asks him three times to reaffirm his love for Him and in doing so recommissions Peter to his calling and ministry. Jesus as the true shepherd (John 10: 11, 14) appoints Peter and other apostles to be subordinate shepherds. Peter will demonstrate his commitment and newly declared love to Jesus by loving God's people in "feeding" them with His Word. Feeding our congregation with Scripture every week is like opening a lunch box, retrieving from it not only what is wholesome and good for growth development, but also a treat that will make them want to come back for more. Preparing weekly sermons and feeding it to those that are committed to our ministry are nothing less than an act of love to Jesus who has called us to take care of those that he has entrusted to us.

In the Gospel of Matthew we read Jesus saying:[6]

52 *"Therefore every teacher of the law who has become a disciple in the kingdom of heaven is like the owner of a house who brings out of his storeroom (treasure room) new treasures as well as old."*

Being able to feed our congregation a 'well balanced diet' is important. If the Word of God is like a treasure house to us, where we reside and spent time at, then it will be possible to grow in understanding in both the new revelation (New Testament) from Jesus and how it fulfils the old promises in the Old Testament. Preaching all of Scripture and not only following our personal canon in The Canon will bring forth an adult like congregation and enrich those under our teaching.

---

[6] Matthew 13:52 New International Version (NIV)

FIXING WHAT IS BROKEN:

Calvin Miller[7] wrote the following in reminding us of the importance of producing sermons that matter and that it is God's intention of using those minutes spent preaching to do the impossible:

We who call ourselves preachers have been called to put it all back together again, one sermon at a time. It is wearisome work. Generations upon centuries of preachers have worked on the list, decade after decade, and then they die and nothing much ever changes. But the work is not futile; the work is the most important work there is. Without our calling (to preach) God's dream of restoring Eden is hopeless. I am a repairman, and the world, as I said, is broken. The only tools in my toolbox are the Book and the sermons I write to take it to the people.

Paul's[8] instruction to young Timothy, in taking on the responsibility of preaching and teaching, is very clear in why it matters to take scripture serious in "repairing" what is broken: "*All Scripture is God-breathed and is useful for teaching, rebuking, correcting and training in righteousness, so that the servant of God may be thoroughly equipped for every good work.*"

Paul stresses the authoritativeness of all Scripture and its usefulness in training those that will fix our broken, shattered and fragmented lives. In a very specific sense, this supports the doctrine of the sufficiency of Scripture, in that the truth contained in Scripture is sufficient in all matters pertaining to doctrine and moral behaviour.

Where the *lunch box* represents the sermon in it is finalised and polished form ready to be fed to the 'sheep', the *toolbox* represents the Bible to be used in all matters and situations that asks for a Godly intervention.

[7] Calvin Miller, *Letters to a Young Pastor* (Colorado Springs: C. Cook Publishers, 2011).

[8] 2 Timothy 3:16-17 *New International Version (NIV)*

GOD LOVES TO SURPRISE HIS SERVANTS!

EZEKIEL ARE GIVEN A SERMON[9]

9 Then I looked, and I saw a hand stretched out to me. In it was a scroll[10] which he unrolled before me. On both sides of it were written words of lament and mourning and woe.

3 And he said to me, "Son of man, eat what is before you, eat this scroll; then go and speak to the people of Israel." 2 So I opened my mouth, and he gave me the scroll to eat.

3 Then he said to me, "Son of man, eat this scroll I am giving you and fill your stomach with it." So I ate it, and it tasted as sweet as honey in my mouth.

4 He then said to me: "Son of man, go now to the people of Israel and speak my words to them."

Ezekiel prophesied during a time of great confusion. In 597 B.C. the Babylonians had exiled Judah's king Jehoiachin along with several thousand of its leading citizens. Ezekiel was among their number. The political situation was indeed complex. The pattern in

---

[9] Ezekiel 2:9-3:4 New International Version (NIV)

the history of Biblical exiles was that prophets emerged in times of testing and crisis to bring God's message to his people.

Ezekiel are *given* a sermon to present to the people of Israel. I do believe that the sermons we as ministers and pastors present to our congregations are in essence in its final form not our insight and creation, but given us in mind and spirit by God Himself. We are to speak God's word to our people and therefore we can expect from God to provide the content we need to talk on just as he provided a scroll to Ezekiel with written words on. The command to eat is combined with the commission to go and speak. When God calls those that have to speak on his behalf he also commissions them with his authority and seal of approval. Finally, having tasted, the prophet gets another surprise: the words of mourning are bitter, as one would expect, but sweet as honey! No matter what Scripture we have to deliver to feed our flock or to fix a wrong perception, when we study the passage "given" to us by the Spirit of God and "eat it"- break it down to bite size- to eventually "fill our stomach" – deal with it until we know that we have studied the passage from all sides and have examined it through and through, we will in preaching that word be left with a sense of obedience and accomplishment. The content may be bitter, but the taste of honey will be our reward!

"How sweet are your words to my taste,
sweeter than honey to my mouth!"[10]

[10] Psalm 119:103 New International Version (NIV)

THE HOLY SPIRIT LOVES TO SURPRISE THE CHURCH

THE POST RESURRECTION FOLLOWERS OF JESUS ARE GIVEN BOLDNESS TO PREACH[11]

"When the day of Pentecost came, they were all together in one place.[2] Suddenly a sound like the blowing of a violent wind came from heaven and filled the whole house where they were sitting. [3] They saw what seemed to be tongues of fire that separated and came to rest on each of them. [4] All of them were filled with the Holy Spirit and began to speak in other tongues ***(languages)***[12] *as the Spirit enabled them.*

[5] Now there were staying in Jerusalem God-fearing Jews from every nation under heaven. [6] When they heard this sound, a crowd came together in bewilderment, because each one heard their own language being spoken. [7] Utterly amazed, they asked: 'Aren't all these who are speaking Galileans? [8] Then how is it that each of us hears them in our native language? [9] Parthians, Medes and Elamites; residents of Mesopotamia, Judea and Cappadocia, Pontus and Asia, [10] Phrygia and Pamphylia, Egypt and the

[11] Acts 2:1-12 New International Version (NIV)

[12] Γλώσσαις: an utterance having the form of language. Most scholars assume that the phenomena described in Acts 2:4 are significantly different from that in 1 Cor. 14:2 in that in one instance people understood in their own regional language what was said.

parts of Libya near Cyrene; visitors from Rome [11] *(both Jews and converts to Judaism); Cretans and Arabs—we hear them declaring the wonders of God in our own tongues!'* [12] *Amazed and perplexed, they asked one another, "What does this mean?"*

The word translated "tongues" can also be translated "languages" and that is the sense that it has in this context. In this case the other languages were understood by various people present in Jerusalem at that time. This is clearly a miracle of speaking for the disciples began "to speak" (preach) about the "mighty works of God" in different regional and International languages. The presence of the crowds indicates that the setting must be the temple grounds, the only place in Jerusalem that could accommodate more than 3000 people. The list of nations demonstrates that already at Pentecost the Christian witness would start and go forth by speaking and witnessing of the great and mighty works of God.

The question remains: *What does this mean?* The purpose of Pentecost was not to make the Church more "Pentecostal", but to move the Church to be speaking participants in "declaring the wonders of God!" The Church will not be in crisis, because some do not speak in tongues or perform supernatural miracles. The Church is in crisis when the world do not hear us speak and witness about the great works of God: Salvation to all in the name of Jesus Christ. Therefore, the Holy Spirit was given to the Church in filling us with courage and boldness in going forth with a message of hope.

HOW TO BECOME AN AGENT OF SURPRISE?

On television there is this eye catching advert that carriers the theme of surprising one's children with a Kinder-chocolate. This is a chocolate in the shape of a chocolate Easter egg with a small surprise toy inside. Parents are encouraged to buy this as a gift that not only surprise kids with a great chocolate taste, but also with the surprise in biting through the chocolate layer in finding a plastic toy! I love this advert, because it not only tells us that children love sugar and an unexpected toy, but they love surprises! Full stop! This does not change all that much in growing old. The sugar may have to go for health reasons and the "toys" we have gathered during our lifetime may have to be given away or sold. But to be surprised is what makes life interesting, no matter our age.

I do believe that in executing our Sunday sermon, something extraordinary is supposed to happen. It is nothing less than when the Holy Spirit, in blessing each member of your church, shares a "Kinder chocolate" moment with those in the pews. Surprise them in revealing not only the sweet relevant honey taste of God's truth, but especially how Christ and his salvation, in surprising ways, are "hidden" away in Scripture once we manage to break through the obvious layer.

MINUTES THAT MATTER:

The following are four criteria to put into practice when seeking God's guidance in constructing a sermon. Time spent in praying, preparation, producing the sermon and proclaiming the message is never wasted time and a constructive way to commit ourselves to the ministry of the Word.

PRAY:

Seeking God in prayer before we start with preparing the sermon is nothing less than an act of humbling ourselves. Before we dig into the word of God we need to humble ourselves in the presence of The WORD. Praying for guidance and in so doing placing our intellect, understanding and pre conceptions on the altar is a testimony of our dependence on the Holy Spirit to reveal to us his truth.

PREPARE:

Spending time in researching the specific Scripture for the coming Sunday is not less spiritual than spending time in prayer before starting the preparation phase. Becoming a rabbi in the Jewish tradition is not only a dedication of many years of preparation, but a personal choice and attitude of staying a student for all your life. Their calling is nothing less than a life committed to studying and reading. Never stop reading and reflecting. Such is the service of the preacher to God.

PRODUCE:

I have a policy that I do not consider the sermon to be done and completed until the Sunday morning prior before leaving for church. On numerous occasions God would enlighten my mind and spirit through a dream at night, an unexpected insight just before waking up the Sunday morning or even reading through my sermon a final time before church. Produce your sermon to be "open ended". Meaning, that you always allow the Holy Spirit to have the last word. Honour the Holy Spirit in all your preparation in always releasing the Word He gave you, back to Him.

PROCLAIM:

Finally it is time to allow the Holy Spirit to surprise the congregation as He has surprised you in revealing the relevant truth as revealed in Scripture. We all have different styles and personalities that enable us to preach and release God's truth in a manner that is authentic to who we are. Trying to follow the style of successful TV preachers and those with full auditoriums are no proof of being faithful to God, when we are not to ourselves. Preach the word and proclaim the message to surprise and when done step away from what you have faithfully released to be God's word for His people. Leave the result to God.

SERMONS FOR FEEDING THE FLOCK

PREACHING AS PASTORAL CARE

IN AGREEMENT WITH GOD - Hebrew 4:12-13

INTRODUCTION:

Question:

Who do you think does Evil fear most?

- A Spirit filled believer?
- Those who come into agreement with God's word?
- An active member of the Church?
- Church leadership?
- A student of the Bible?

CONTENT:

Read Dt. 19:15 and 1Ti 5:19

Deuteronomy 19:15

"*One witness is not enough to convict anyone accused of any crime or offense they may have committed. A matter must be established by the testimony of two or three witnesses.*"

1 Timothy 5:19

"*Do not entertain an accusation against an elder unless it is brought by two or three witnesses.*"

In Scripture we find the above important principle when dealing with conflict and disagreement in our congregations. These scriptures were given as an instruction in the Old Testament and followed through into the New Testament. Only when 2 or 3 people were in agreement with one another (their individual versions of the facts or story lined up 100%) could it be established as the truth of the matter. The principle of authority which comes from the right kind of alignment or association is what is described here.

Hebrews 4:12-13

"For the word of God is alive and active. Sharper than any double-edged sword, it penetrates even to dividing soul and spirit, joints and marrow; it judges the thoughts and attitudes of the heart. Nothing in all creation is hidden from God's sight. Everything is uncovered and laid bare before the eyes of him to whom we must give account."

"For the word of God is alive and active." How did creation, according to the Biblical witness, came into being? God spoke actively, creatively and intentionally into bringing forth creation. Thus giving it a life of its own (Ge 1:3, 6, 9, 11, 14, 20, 24, 26, and 29). We serve a speaking God: *"…man does not live on bread alone but on every word that comes from the mouth of God." (Dt. 8:3).*

According to Hebrews 4:12 God's speech (his spoken word) is sharper than any *"double-edged"* sword. *Double-edged = Di-stomon (Greek New Testament):*

- *Di = 2*
- *Stomon = mouth*
- *TWO MOUTHED SWORD!*

With Jesus being tested by Satan in the wilderness we find a practical explanation for the above. According to Luke 4:1-13 Satan tested Jesus when Jesus had already fasted for 40 days. Satan appealed to Jesus human nature by tempting Him with *food (flesh), fame and fate*. How did Jesus, resist Satan? He used the *"two mouthed sword."* He came into agreement with what is written in the word of God. He voiced what was already prior voiced by God in the book of Deuteronomy. As Jesus repeated what God had already revealed about Himself –putting his voice with his Fathers voice, confirming what was already spoken by His heavenly Father (2 or 3 witnesses from Dt 19:15), Satan backed off. Jesus countered Satan's attack on Him by quoting from the book of Deuteronomy:

- Man shall not live on bread alone = Dt 8:3
- Worship the Lord your God and serve Him only = Dt 6:13
- Do not put the Lord your God to the test = Dt 6:16

God spoke these words according to Deuteronomy 1:3 through Moses and Jesus put His voice to it and because of the agreement between the Father and Son, these words became a two edged sword- extremely dangerous, making the enemy flee. The secret of resisting Evil and its coming against us is by putting our voice to Scripture and speaking it in agreement! Just as Jesus did!

Confession of sin:

1 John 1:8-10

"If we claim to be without sin, we deceive ourselves and the truth is not in us. [9] If we confess our sins, he is faithful and just and will forgive us our sins and purify us from all unrighteousness. [10] If we claim we have not sinned, we make him out to be a liar and his word is not in us."

Confessing our sin before God works in the same manner and with the same principle in mind. In 1 John 1: 8-10. The word: *confession* in the Greek language has the meaning of: *Coming into agreement with God.* When the Holy Spirit convicts us of sin and we confess our wrong doing, we come into agreement with the Holy Spirit and can Evil no longer keep us in bondage. As soon as we agree with the word that we were in the wrong, darkness cannot prevail. Then we come under the righteousness of God as no power can stand against the "two-mouthed sword."

CLOSING:

Who do you think Evil fear most?

Those who understand the authority of God to protect us against- and to free us from sin, when we align ourselves with the word of God and dare to speak it in agreement with His will.

NOTES:

....

....

....

....

....

....

....

....

....

....

BAPTISM – A MEANS TO AN END OR A GODLY INITIATIVE? John 1:29-34

INTRODUCTION:

The Gospel of Mark was written most probable in the mid 50's AD

The Gospel of Matthew was written most probable in the late 50's AD

The Gospel of Luke was written most probable in the early 60's AD

The Gospel of John was written after 70 AD (70-100)

The Gospel of John was written not only last (at a later time) of the Gospels, but also at a time when the Church has now started to function as a Christian institute and not merely as a Jesus movement. The Church has now taken on a fixed form and a specific way of functioning. All considered it has now been, given and taken a little, more than 40 years since Jesus was taken up into glory. Only now does the writer of the Gospel of John decide to write his version and interpretation of Jesus and his ministry. But it is more than just another witness to the life and ministry of Jesus…the author is looking critical at the way that the early Church has become more focused on ceremony and religion than on the work of the Holy Spirit.

CONTENT:

John 1:29-34

29 The next day John saw Jesus coming toward him and said, "Look, the
Lamb of God, who takes away the sin of the world! 30 This is the one I
meant when I said, 'A man who comes after me has surpassed me because
he was before me.' 31 I myself did not know him, but the reason I came
baptizing with water was that he might be revealed to Israel."

32 Then John gave this testimony: "I saw the Spirit come down from
heaven as a dove and remain on him. 33 And I myself did not know
him, but the one who sent me to baptize with water told me, 'The man
on whom you see the Spirit come down and remain is the one who will
baptize with the Holy Spirit.' 34 I have seen and I testify that this is God's
Chosen One."

In all the other previous Gospels (Mark, Matthew, Luke) it is mentioned or implied that John the Baptist baptised Jesus. The writer of John gospel does not follow the same line of interpretation. According to his version there is no mention that John the Baptised actively baptised Jesus. Rather he focuses on the overwhelming presence of the Holy Spirit and His partnership with the Father in releasing Jesus to start his public ministry (John 1:43). *Why does John not mention any human agent baptising Jesus? Why does he intentionally not mention John the Baptist baptising Jesus?*

In the early stages of the development of the Christian Church people started to take on prominent roles in the church. Unfortunately, it seems that the mediation of the Church and the clergy became so prominent that the author of John's Gospel feared that man's role in the Church became more prominent than God's initiative. He therefore does not acknowledge Jesus baptism as the work of a man, but rather the powerful intervention of the Spirit of God. The same happens in chapter 3, where the author does not acknowledge that people find salvation by means of the intervention of the Church or its clever teachers, but by the powerful work of the Holy Spirit (John 3:5-8)!

Although, the Church is called to practice the ministry of baptism and to adhere to Jesus command to baptise those coming to faith and joining the church, it is the outworking of the Holy Spirit and His agenda towards the one that is being baptised that is of importance. Who the person is that is administrating the baptism does not matter (that minister can even leave his calling and the church the Monday after he had baptised you)…that will not make any difference to God welcoming you into the Body of believers and blessing you with the companionship of the Holy Spirit on your new journey. *THE BLESSING OF BAPTISM IS NOT THE RESULT OF MAN'S DOING, BUT THE OUTWORKING OF THE GRACE OF GOD!*

- Baptism in itself does NOT SAVE OUR SOULS FOR ETERNITY (Faith in Jesus Christ does), because it is a *SIGN*. A sign to the Church and to the one who is baptised...
- That God has decided to commit Himself to me (John 1:32).
- That God has decided to invest His Kingdom in me (John 1:33).
- That God has decided to choose me (John 1:34).
- Baptism is a *SEAL:*
  In ancient times a king would take his ring and make a print of the seal on it, by using candle wax to seal a document with his authority and to proof that he is the author of the content. This is a legal indication that he authorise whatever is mentioned in the treaty or contract. Baptism functions as such a seal whereby God declares on the day of our baptism:
- That He puts his "stamp of approval" on my life, because of the righteousness that I receive from Jesus sacrificial death.
- That He himself authorises my membership of the body of Christ (Universal Church).
- That I shall from now onwards not live under the authority of sin or the flesh, but under the authority of the Spirit.

According to Romans 6:1-14

- SIN DOES NOT DEFINE WHO WE ARE – WE CAN DEAL WITH OUR PAST (Rom. 6: 1-7). Baptism is a sign of what happens when we come to faith in Christ. We are forgiven and cleansed from all the stains of our past.

- DEATH DOES NOT HOLD US CAPTIVE ANY LONGER – WE CAN DEAL WITH OUR FUTURE (Rom. 6:8-10). Baptism is a sign of what we believe about the future…that death will not hold us captive, but that we will be resurrected from death unto everlasting life with Jesus. We will have an eternal future to spend with Him.
- THE LAW OF GOD, WHEN PRACTISED AS RELIGION, CANNOT FIND US GUILTY AS CHARGED – BECAUSE THE LIFE WE NOW LIVE IS UNDER THE PROTECTION OF GRACE – WE CAN DEAL WITH THE PRESENT (Rom.6:14). After we come to faith and are baptised God is not done with us… he bestows His grace upon us every day so that we can move into His purpose for our lives.

CLOSING:

IF BAPTISM CONFIRMS THAT SIN DOES NOT DEFINE US, DEATH DOES NOT HOLD US AND RELIGION DOES NOT OWN US….TO WHOM DO WE BELONG? JESUS! You now fully belong to Jesus…and that is why you cannot submit to sin or please man…you are now under obligation to serve Jesus as your Saviour and MASTER-Rom.6:11-13.

NOTES:

....

....

....

....

....

....

....

COMMUNION - Luke 24:13-35

INTRODUCTION:

The Agape Feast (love feast) among the early Christians developed into a more formal ministry called the Eucharist (*Eucharisto*) which means to be *grateful or to give thanks.* Communion (so called in Protestant churches) is one of the Sacraments that is linked to Baptism. Where baptism is a once of sacrament we find that communion is a regular celebration of thanks giving.

A Sacrament is a SIGN that points to some crucial aspects in the life of the people of God.

CONTENT:

Communion is a *sign of our deliverance from the wrath of God.* Communion calls us into remembrance of not only being saved by God in Jesus Christ, but also being saved from God who is holy and righteous!

Exodus 12:12-14

12 "On that same night I will pass through Egypt and strike down every firstborn of both people and animals, and I will bring judgment on all the gods of Egypt. I am the LORD.
13 The blood will be a sign for you on

the houses where you are, and when I see the blood, I will pass over you. No destructive plague will touch you when I strike Egypt.

14 "This is a day you are to commemorate; for the generations to come you shall celebrate it as a festival to the LORD—a lasting ordinance."

Communion reminds us that as the blood of the Passover lamb on the doorpost of Israel's dwellings delivered Israel from the death of every first born son in Egypt, so has the blood of Jesus on the cross saved us from the wrath of God!

Luke 24:25-27

25 He said to them, "How foolish you are, and how slow to believe all that the prophets have spoken! 26 Did not the Messiah have to suffer these things and then enter his glory?" 27 And beginning with Moses and all the Prophets, he explained to them what was said in all the Scriptures concerning himself.

We find Jesus, after His resurrection, reminding the two men travelling to Emmaus of the redemptive work of God as it was revealed in Scripture (Luke 24:25-27).

Communion is also a sign of God being present among us and journeying with us in this life. God has not left us to our own devices as these two men thought. No! Communion wants to reveal to us that Jesus has been the one journeying with us all along! (Luke 24:30-32).

Communion finally encourage us to take on the future! It gives us hope! These two men immediately set out to witness to the other eleven disciples and to encourage them (Luke 24:33-35). Communion launches us into the community and the world as bearers of HOPE!

CLOSING:[13]

In the Babylonian Talmud, we find a commentary on our specific Scripture reading in *Luke* 24:13-35. The Talmud says: "The host should break bread" (Berakoth 46). In Jewish tradition, the host – the head of the household – is the one who always says the blessing and breaks the bread. Strangers who are invited to the meal usually

[13] eTeacher Biblical – Israel Academy of Language and History.

wait for directions from their host and quietly receive what is set before them.

However, that is not what we see here (Luke 24:30-31). Clearly this was not a regular guest! Instead of waiting for his host's direction, this stranger (Jesus) is taking the host's place: He is saying the blessing and breaking the bread! We can imagine that this behaviour must have caught the attention of everyone in the house. Where did this authority come from?

Here I would like to quote a passage from the Dead Sea Scrolls. The Qumran Sectarians seemed to believe in the *Eternal Saviour* (they believed it was Melchizedek), who would come as man and was known to them as the Teacher of Righteousness. The Teacher of Righteousness was a priest. Let us have a look on a fragmentary document 1QSa (sometimes called *The Messianic Rule*) and see what this text says about the Priest; *[the Messiah of Israel shall [enter] … and* ***[no-one should stretch out]*** *his hand to the first fruit … before the Priest, for [he is the one who blesses the first-fruit of the bread and of the new wine … … (column 2, lines 18-21).*

'No-one should stretch out his hand to bless the bread'**:** it means that, in the time of the coming Messiah, there was an understanding that when the Messiah arrives, no-one should stretch out his hand to bless the bread before Him. The authority to bless the bread first clearly belonged to the host – or to the Messiah. And when, in our story, this stranger acted in the house as *one that had authority,* we can imagine that, even though the eyes of the disciples were still restrained, their hearts that had been burning along the way were now filled with excitement and anticipation. Jesus behaviour was a definite sign to them of His messianic personality.

May we "see" Jesus in serving us - and sharing with us communion at his table of grace?

NOTES:

....

....

....

....

....

....

....

....

....

....

THE REVELATION OF THE **DOVE** – Genesis. 7:1-5/7:17-22/8:6-17 and Matthew 3:13-17

INTRODUCTION:

Resilience is one of the great characteristics of humans! We have the ability to overcome. Human history is full of evidence with many examples. The Jewish nation is one in not only surviving the holocaust, but in 1948 declaring themselves to be the nation of Israel in occupying land. Becoming the youngest and most modern country state in the world. Europe in rebuilding its past and rich history after two devastating World Wars is another example of resilience. In general we only need to acknowledge countries and individuals which often started from scratch after surviving natural disasters like floods, earth quakes and hurricanes. The Biblical story of Noah and his family being sole survivors after God's devastating judgement on creation tops the scale in regards to human resilience. They not only survived an epic flood, but had to be instrumental in Gods' actions of re-creating the world.

CONTENT:

Read Genesis 7:1-5/17-23/8:1-17

The raven was sent by Noah, from the Ark, to find if proper land can be spotted in spite of the water still residing, but it does not return with any proof of new life…finding only a resting place on the mountain tops and feeding on carcasses. The dove, in comparison with the raven, returned after its second journey with a fresh plucked olive leaf! An indication that the land was drying, but more importantly that *new life* was taking place – a new creation was on its way! A fresh start at last! (The repeated use of the number 7 reminds us of the Genesis creation account where God created the universe during the duration of 7 days).

Matthew 3:13-17

[16] As soon as Jesus was baptized, he went up out of the water. At that moment heaven was opened, and he saw the Spirit of God descending like a dove and alighting on him. [17] And a voice from heaven said, "This is my Son, whom I love; with him I am well pleased."

In the New Testament the Holy Spirit is symbolised by a dove. In this context the Spirit of God anoints Jesus as Israel's King and commissions Him as God's righteous servant. In other words: the dove as a physical symbol of the Holy Spirit is very much a symbol of God's stamp of approval-approving what Jesus is about to set out to accomplish - establishing the Kingdom of God on earth.

What is the important connection between the dove in the story of Noah and the dove in the story of Jesus induction as the righteous servant of God?

- The dove in the Genesis story – returning with the olive leaf –symbolised *new life*. Jesus would bring new spiritual life to the people of Israel and eternal life to all.
- The dove returning with the olive leaf symbolised a *new start* for mankind and a new future for all of creation. Jesus makes it possible for mankind to make a fresh start as he forgives us our sin and makes us righteous in God's site. In Jesus we have a new future – even an *everlasting future*!
- The Holy Spirit is longing to release the people of God into a new season and a fresh calling. The Spirit of God is longing

to bring us out of previous seasons and circumstances to empower us *to do a new thing for God!*

CLOSING:

In the Noah story it is the dove that brings joy and hope to the survivors in the Ark. In seeing the olive leave that the dove brought back, it indicated that God did not forget Noah and his family. God was indeed keeping to his promise of a new creation and a new start. With Jesus baptism and consecration (by the divine intervention of the Father and the empowerment thereof through the endorsement of the Holy Spirit in the form of a dove) was it confirmed that God did not forget about fallen humanity. The Son of God indeed arrived to restore peach between God and man.

NOTES:

....

....

....

....

....

....

....

....

....

....

ELDERSHIP – Acts 20:13-38

INTRODUCTION:

Paul is traveling through Greece on his way to Jerusalem to be in time for the feast of Pentecost. Having spent three years in Ephesus, Paul knew he would be delayed with too many farewells there, so he chose to sail past the city so that he could reach Jerusalem in time.

CONTENT:

A PASTOR TO THE PASTOR:

In spite of Paul being in a hurry to reach Jerusalem he sent a message to the elders in Ephesus to meet him in one of the four harbours in Miletus. Why would Paul do this knowing that he had a tight schedule? Paul is under extreme pressure and concerned about what awaits him when he reaches Jerusalem (verse 22-23). He needs the support and encouragement of his elders. Being in ministry can be a very lonely and frightening experience. In speaking to graduating pastors, Calvin Miller shares the following in his book, *Letters to young pastors*: *"Most of you will be taking churches of 100 members or less. Twenty years from now, 80% of you will no longer be a pastor, having chosen another profession primarily because the pain of hanging on was greater than the risk of letting go. 20% of you who have continued preaching will still be in churches of 100 members or less... happy graduation!"*

Paul wanted to stay true to his calling no matter what he had to face, but needed to confine in his trusted elders. ELDERS ARE CALLED TO SUPPORT THEIR PASTOR! Elders are called to be a PASTOR TO THEIR PASTOR (verse 37 mentions 4 powerful words that is characteristic of pastoral care: "wept", "embraced", "kissed" and "accompanied").

PROTECT THE PARISH:

Being a wolf is a matter of the heart, not of outward appearance. That's why Jesus warned about wolves that come in sheep's clothing (Matt. 7:15). It takes a fair amount of discernment for a sheep to recognize that this isn't another sheep; it's a wolf! Paul calls them "angels of light," disguised as "servants of righteousness." But then he adds, "whose' end will be according to their deeds" (2 Cor. 11:14-15). Their evil deeds expose them for what they really are, false teachers, wolves in sheep's clothing, who are out for personal glory and gain, not for the glory of Christ.

In his book, *A Shepherd Looks at Psalm 23*, Phillip Keller says that he has heard of two dogs that killed 292 sheep in a single night of unbridled slaughter. One morning at dawn, he found nine of his choicest ewes, all soon to lamb, lying dead after a cougar had attacked the flock in the night. From then on, he slept with a loaded rifle and flashlight near his bed. At the least sound, he would leap from bed and dash out into the night to protect his sheep. That is a picture of the job of godly elders. Because the flock is precious to God, since He purchased it with the blood of His own Son, elders must guard it from spiritual wolves that would destroy and wound the flock, especially the lambs.

DO NOT ONLY PREACH IN PART:

Paul writes to Timothy in 2 Timothy 3:14-17 on the importance of the above. Elders are called to not only preach on their preferred theological themes, but all of the Scriptures. We all have Biblical themes and topics that we are really into which excites us in our Christian walk. Elders however need to be disciplined to preach not only their agenda-topics, but that which is contextual and at the same time in obedience to the voice and guidance of the Holy Spirit. Elders have a responsibility to know the Bible, but even more importantly to love the content of God's revelation in his Word.

CLOSING:

Finally, Paul can now focus on his calling to leave for Jerusalem knowing that he has committed, the elders that he trained for 3 years, to God's care and to the guidance of the Word (v.32).

These Elders were ready…

…to care for their future pastor

…to care for the parish

…to care for the preaching

NOTES:

....

....

....

....

....

....

....

....

....

....

BACK TO THE **FUTURE** – Genesis 22

INTRODUCTION:

Human sacrifice was not unknown in the Ancient Near East (ANE), though early examples of it are rare.

Philo of Byblos says that the Phoenicians had an ancient custom: "they offered their dearest children in a way full of mystery" when danger threatened the nation. In Bible times, the King of Moab offered his son as a burnt offering when his capital was under siege (2 Kings 3:27).

This Canaanite and Phoenician practice came into Israel under apostate kings when Ahaz "made his son pass through the fire" (2 Kings 16:3) and Manasseh did the same (2 Kings 21:6). The custom was probably fairly widespread, since it prompted condemnations of the practice in the Bible (Leviticus 18:21; 20:2-5; Deuteronomy 18:10; 2 Kings 17:17; 21:6; 2 Chronicles 28:3; 23:10; Psalm 106:37-38; Jeremiah 19:4-5; 32:35).

But, Abraham didn't have the benefit of God's revelation to Moses and the prophets, of the Old Testament scriptures. All he knew was that child sacrifice was practiced by some of the Canaanites. Instead of being morally incensed by the practice (as we are, with our knowledge of God's revealed will), Abraham had no option but to believe that God seriously demanded that he sacrifice his son as a "burnt offering," that is, a sacrifice that is fully consumed by the fire upon the altar.

CONTENT:

The correlation between Genesis 22 and the substitutionary atonement of Jesus Christ is striking:

- Gn. 22:2 in relation to John.3:16 – Abraham sacrificing Isaac and God willing for His Son, Jesus to die on a cross.
- The donkey in Gn. 22:3 that carries Isaac to Moriah corresponds with Jesus riding on a donkey when He enters Jerusalem on His way to Golgotha in Mt. 21:1-5.
- Isaac carried the wood for the burnt offering in Gn.22:6 on his back which corresponds with Jesus carrying the wooden cross on his back according to John 19:17.
- The 3rd day as mentioned in Gn. 22:4 corresponds with Jesus being resurrected on the 3rd day.
- Abraham offered Isaac on mount Moriah which is the mount on which the Jerusalem temple was built and therefore in the proximity of Golgotha where Jesus would die much later.

Genesis 22 therefore functions as a modern day billboard, advertising the COMING SOON event of the death and resurrection of Jesus Christ! Genesis 22 describes a future prophetic event, in revealing the salvation and substitutionary atonement of Jesus Christ that was to come.

When Abraham prepared to offer Isaac on the altar, he was in actual fact preparing to offer his own FUTURE! In the Old Near East you did not have a retirement package, as we all are inclined to have today. In the Old Near Eastern culture your sons were your security and retirement plan. Your sons would care and provide for you. The more sons you had the more attractive your retirement package would be. Having no sons meant that your financial security in your old age would not come too much. Your sons is summoned to care for you. Abraham only had Isaac (Ishmael was not his biological son) so when God commanded him to sacrifice Isaac God was asking

Abraham to offer his future to God. To trust God to such an extent that He was willing to put his future in God's hands!

CLOSING:

It is not much of a commitment to offer our past to God. If you are anything like me you have also made your share of mistakes and have happily given God your sinful past. Not a problem....love to get rid of that kind of bad past that ties you down and enslaves you. But giving God your future is huge...it is nothing less than denying yourself!

This reminds me of the story of the Pig and the Chicken. Both these animals lived on a farm. They enjoyed the comfort of the country life, but felt constrained because both of them had an adventurous personality. One day finally they decided to jump the fence and run for the bypass road into town. Before sunrise they were of. Excited to see and experience town life. Many hours later on entering the town they realised that both of them were hungry. Walking down the main street they soon found a restaurant with a notice saying: *BREAKFAST SPECIAL TODAY: Bacon and eggs!*

In a flash the chicken entered the restaurant, but the pig remained outside! As both animals had no money to pay for breakfast the pig realised that the chicken would manage by laying a few eggs to compensate for being broke. He, the pig, on the other hand would have to offer his life and his whole existence to replace the meal. He would become the next bacon!

Giving God our past is what God's grace allows us to do. Giving God our future is what faith invites us to do!

NOTES:

....

....

....

....

GODS **GLOBAL** ECONOMY – Exodus 16

INTRODUCTION:

When one finds oneself in a place or situation of being *in between* or in a state of *transformation* it seems uncomfortable and uncertain. Israel has recently escaped from Egypt which was familiar to them for the duration of 400 years! They find it hard to change from being slave workers in Egypt to adventure seekers out in the dessert. Although they were slaves in Egypt they had a fixed address and meat to eat! Now they are free, but what is so great about that if you are sent into the dessert to starve? What Israel did not realise was that the dessert would teach them the principles of God's global economy.

CONTENT:

GOD KNOWS OUR NEEDS: Ex.16:17-18.

Moses said to them, "It is the bread the LORD HAS GIVEN YOU TO EAT.[16]
This is what the LORD HAS COMMANDED: 'EVERYONE IS TO GATHER AS MUCH AS THEY NEED. TAKE AN *omer ('a scoop')* for each person you have in your tent.'"

[17] *The Israelites did as they were told; some gathered much, some little.*[18]
And when they measured it by the omer, the one who gathered much

did not have too much, and the one who gathered little did not have too little. Everyone had gathered just as much as they needed.

God's provision is always sufficient for my unique circumstances. It is wrong to try and measure God by too much, or too little, because God deals with each and every one of us in regards to what we *need*! Matthew 6:31-32 confirms this principle when it says: *"So do not worry, saying 'What shall we eat?' or 'What shall we drink?' or 'What shall we wear?' For the pagans run after all these things, and your heavenly Father knows that you need them."*

GOD'S PROVISION IS ON A DAILY BASIS: Ex.16:19-20.

Then Moses said to them, "No one is to keep any of it until morning."

20 However, some of them paid no attention to Moses; they kept part of it until morning, but it was full of maggots and began to smell. So Moses was angry with them.

God's provision is so reliable that we can count on it every day. *GOD IS INTO SUSTAINABILITY*! Providing continuously.

WHY WERE ISRAEL NOT SUPPOSE TO GATHER FOOD ON THE SABBATH? Ex.16:23-26

He said to them, "This is what the LORD COMMANDED: 'Tomorrow is to be a day of Sabbath rest, a holy Sabbath to the LORD. SO BAKE WHAT YOU WANT TO BAKE AND BOIL WHAT YOU WANT TO BOIL. SAVE WHATEVER IS LEFT AND KEEP IT UNTIL MORNING.'"

24 So they saved it until morning, as Moses commanded, and it did not stink or get maggots in it. 25 "Eat it today," Moses said, "because today is a Sabbath to the LORD. YOU WILL NOT FIND ANY OF IT ON THE GROUND TODAY. 26 Six days you are to gather it, but on the seventh day, the Sabbath, there will not be any."

God wanted Israel to acknowledge that material incentives is not there reel need. There biggest need is God himself. More than we need to be sustained by what God provides for us, we need HIM even more! Israel had to realise that in God's Global Economy God is to be worshipped not for His ability to provide, nor for His sustainability, but primarily because life itself is a gracious gift from

Him. The Sabbath and keeping to its laws would help the Israelites acknowledge that God is greater than his ability to provide. God is the subject of their worship because he chose them as his people!

GODS PROVISION IS ALSO FOR OUR CHILDREN Ex.16:31-33.

[31] The people of Israel called the bread manna. It was white like coriander seed and tasted like wafers made with honey. [32] Moses said, "This is what the LORD HAS COMMANDED: 'TAKE AN *omer of manna and keep it for the generations to come, so they can see the bread I gave you to eat in the wilderness when I brought you out of Egypt.'"*

[33] So Moses said to Aaron, "Take a jar and put an omer of manna in it. Then place it before the LORD TO BE KEPT FOR THE GENERATIONS TO COME."

Moses ordered that a jar of manna be placed inside the Golden Ark that was in the tabernacle. This would be a visual reminder to the next generation that God is indeed able to create and supply food to his people even in harsh places such as a dessert. God's intention was to not only support and provide for the current Israelites, but for the future generations as well. There is no restrictions on God's ability to provide. God is in the business of providing for his Church – for the long haul!

CLOSING:

At last God changed the menu for Israel after 40 years, as they settled into Canaan. Once they reached the border of Canaan the provision of Manna stopped. They would now start cultivating the land as Israel would in time change their lifestyle from nomads to farming and producing food from the fertile valleys that they are about to invade. God's global economic principles do include hard work: First they would have to fight to gain land as promised by God and then secondly develop and cultivate what God has entrusted and blessed them with. May we always be good stewards and overseers in whatever way God blesses and cares for us from within his global economy?

NOTES:

....

....

....

....

....

....

....

....

....

....

THE HOLINESS OF GOD:
Exodus 20:1-21

INTRODUCTION:

The 10 commandments were given to the Hebrew people to keep them from committing sin and offending God who is Holy and just. It was to help Israel appreciate the fact that God wanted them to serve him not on their terms but on His terms.

The whole Torah (first 5 books of the Old Testament) is based primarily on maintaining a relationship with God who is Holy.

The Old Testament laws and rites can be summarized by Lev.20:26 which reads:

"*You are to be holy to me because I, the LORD, am holy, and I have set you apart from the nations to be my own*".

In our secularised society today we have some voices that are of the opinion that we do not have to live in fear of a holy God as Jesus, God's son, has fully complied with the demands of the 10 Commandments, in living a holy life, and in so doing has gained favour with God on behalf of sinful humanity. They base their understanding on Luke 6:36 which reads:

"Be merciful, just as your Father is merciful."

Has God compromised his holiness with His mercifulness, so that He at least can have subjects that will serve him? Off course not… Jesus himself declares the following in Matthew 5:17-20:

"Do not think that I have come to abolish the Law or the Prophets; I have not come to abolish them but to fulfil them. [18] *For truly I tell you, until heaven and earth disappear, not the smallest letter, not the least stroke of a pen, will by any means disappear from the Law until everything is accomplished.* [19] *Therefore anyone who sets aside one of the least of these commands and teaches others accordingly will be called least in the kingdom of heaven, but whoever practices and teaches these commands will be called great in the kingdom of heaven.* [20] *For I tell you that unless your righteousness surpasses that of the Pharisees and the teachers of the law, you will certainly not enter the kingdom of heaven."*

God's love for us does not override His character which is one of righteousness and holiness.

CONTENT:

Both the Pharisees and Jesus kept God's holiness in high regards and tried to keep people from committing sin and offending God. But the way the Pharisees and Jesus went about accomplishing it were worlds apart.

The Pharisees had developed a system of 613 laws of which 365 where negative commands and 248 positive laws...

These comprehensive religious regulations became a burden to Israel and demanded an almost super human approach to achieve.

Let me explain by making use of an example: For Jews keeping the Sabbath they were not allowed to work. That is the standard law reminding Israel that it is not their labour during the week that makes it possible for them to meet all their needs, but that it is actually God's blessing and grace. By not working one day out of the week they were simply acknowledging God for that. But now the Pharisees made it a huge burden by not allowing the people to cook food as it was considered to be "work".

The Law, against working on the Sabbath day, included travel (see Exodus 16:27-30). The limit set by the rabbis to the Sabbath day's journey was 2,000 cubits from one's house or domicile, which was derived from the statement found in Joshua 3:4 that this was the distance between the ark and the people on their march; this being assumed to be the distance between the tents of the people and the tabernacle during the sojourn in the wilderness. Hence, it must have been allowable to travel thus far to attend the worship of the tabernacle. We do not know when this assumption in regard to the Sabbath day's journey was made, but it seems to have been still in force in the time of Christ, travelling to the temple courts.

Jesus way of dealing with the law was different than the approach of the Pharisees. Where the Pharisees used *STOP signs* to keep the masses intact, Jesus used *"fences"*.[14] A fence in this example is a protective enclosure around a commandment, an extra layer of caution. First one has to scale the protective fence and only then be in a position to transgress the actual holy commandment. This way it will be more difficult for people to transgress the Torah. And as rabbis of his day, Jesus built "fences" around commandments too!

"You have heard that it was said, 'You shall not commit adultery'; but I say to you that everyone who looks at a woman with lust for her has already committed adultery with her in his heart" (Mat 5:27-28).

First Jesus quoted the original commandment (Exodus 20:14) and added *"but I say to you..."* and then comes Jesus' protective fence: "avoid lustful gazing!" According to Jesus wisdom, adultery and unfaithfulness come from looking at someone or something that is not yours, and suddenly the desire is born. Jesus says that this is already a sin. But merely looking at people is not prohibited in Torah – that's a fence. The fence is to avoid inappropriate gazing that leads to inappropriate desires and one will not commit the actual sin of adultery. This is Jesus building a fence around a biblical commandment, just like other rabbis of his day.

[14] eTeacher Biblical – Israel Academy of Language and History.

CLOSING:

The Pharisees intention was good, but the way they enforced the law was a burden and a heavy loud to carry…an even impossible load to carry. In Jesus case he demonstrated the Law of God to be a blessing that protects us and keep us fenced in so that we do not hurt ourselves and others. In Matthew 11:30 Jesus declares that "His yoke is easy and His burden is light." This is seen to be the strategy in how Jesus use the Old Testament law in not only keeping the holiness of God intact, but protecting us from violating the holiness of His character.

NOTES:

……………………………………………………………………………………………

……………………………………………………………………………………………

……………………………………………………………………………………………

……………………………………………………………………………………………

……………………………………………………………………………………………

……………………………………………………………………………………………

……………………………………………………………………………………………

……………………………………………………………………………………………

……………………………………………………………………………………………

……………………………………………………………………………………………

INTOXICATED WITH LSD – Acts 6:1-7

INTRODUCTION:

Question: What makes a church *EFFECTIVE?*

Answer: *LSD (LEADERSHIP, STRUCTURE and DIVINE intervention).*

LSD is a dangerous drug that goes by the street name of Looney Tunes. When druggies are looking for another kind of "out of this world trip" or "experience" they ask for a "FIX". The church is desperately in need of a fix…a different kind of a FIX…an answer…a solution to its everyday existence in being more *effective.*

CONTENT:

The Hellenists were a collective name for Greek speaking (Christian) Jews originating from outside of Palestine. Among these Greek speaking worshippers in the Jerusalem congregation were widows with no significant income and in need of daily food provisions. As the Jerusalem congregation had initially started with 3000 members (Acts 2:41), when it opened its doors and seeing daily growth, the 12 Apostles could not keep up with ministry demands. The church were not effective anymore and people were suffering because of it.

What did the apostles do to FIX this situation? They used LSD!

L*eadership*: Acts 6:3a

They chose men who were known for their faith, wisdom and cooperation with the Holy Spirit. Commissioning the right people for a specific task can make the church more effective.

S*tructure*: Acts 6:3b-4

Getting the structure right is very important to see the church move forward. In Acts 6 this allowed for leaders to get on with what they were good at and called to do in allowing others to do the same. (Elders are called into spiritual leadership/managers are called into the practical and logistical side of supporting the church).

D*ivine intervention*: Acts 6:7

God always use the church to build His kingdom…no matter in what style or size they come, but when a church has an effective leadership and a supportive structure to minister in, we do not need to push and pull so hard to see results:

- The Gospel **message** spread further
- **Membership** increased rapidly
- **Miracles** happened as Jewish orthodox Jews came to faith

CLOSING:

Once in a small town the pastor of a small local church would visit the railway station on his day of. Once a week the pastor would drive to the railway station but would never buy a ticket to go somewhere. He would simply sit down on a bench on the platform as he waited for the steam engine to huff and puff its way through the station, pulling countless trucks behind it. When asked, one day, why he would do this every week on his day of, he answered: "It is always a comfort coming to the station in time to see the locomotive pushing and pulling to get the trucks through the station. This is a reminder that I am not the only one every Sunday trying to push and pull my congregation towards God and away from the world."

Without committed and Spirit filled volunteers in leadership, as well as not having a well thought through system, can make the church use all its energy on pulling and pushing, instead of sharing the message, encouraging membership and rejoicing in the miracles!

NOTES:

....

....

....

....

....

....

....

....

....

....

JESUS IS OUR **JUSTIFICATION** –
Galations.1:1-10/2:15-21

INTRODUCTION:

In secular society the expression "X factor" has a positive ring to it. It means to have a certain advantage above the rest or to be above average. In Galatians chapter 1 Paul addresses an issue that I like to call the + Factor. In those churches that Paul planted in the province of Galatia in 48 AD there were a growing perception that the saving grace of God was not enough for sinners to be saved from their sin and not enough to be set free from their past. *You had to incorporate the + factor. YOU HAD TO ADD TO WHAT JESUS ACHIEVED ON THE CROSS*.

Some that once found salvation in Jesus Christ and once were celebrating their forgiveness as a free gift from God was now deserting this foundational faith and started turning to the + factor. Suddenly the good news of Jesus saving grace were understood not to be sufficient anymore. *Jesus + circumcision saves....Jesus + the Law of Moses saves. Yes Jesus saves, but you also need to do this and you also need to do that...In short: a strange gospel was developing that was teaching that Jesus free gift of forgiveness was not enough...you needed the + factor!*

CONTENT:

Paul is writing to these backsliding Jews in explaining that the salvation that Jesus attained for them on the cross was sufficient. Meaning that Jesus *completed* the task of justification. What he started he finished on our behalf and it was done *perfect,* according to the expectation of Old Testament law. There is no need to add on to the equation!

Some say Jesus + good works ("the works of the Law") saves.

Some say Jesus + service to the church saves.

Some say Jesus + tithing saves.

Some say Jesus + communion saves.

Some say Jesus + baptism saves

That is why Paul reacted in saying in Galatians 2:16

"…Know that a person is not justified by the works of the law, but by faith in Jesus Christ. So we, too, have put our faith in Christ Jesus that we may be justified by faith in Christ and not by the works of the law, because by the works of the law no one will be justified."

In using my own metaphor, Paul was asking the Church: why would you want to add other ingredients to a proven recipe if it is not needed and will compromise the results? Why change a recipe that is bulletproof and always deliver? Why add human ingenuity and human insecurity to the perfect and finalised work of justification through the works of Christ? Why?

According to James 2:14-26, *good works is no requirement to be saved, it is the result of being saved. The fruit thereof.* When you and I accept the salvation and justification of Jesus Christ and realise that the grace that is so freely given to us is absolutely free…we want to life to the glory of God and want to honour Him through a lifestyle of thanks giving!

CLOSING:

It is no coincidence that the shape of the tree that Jesus died on was in the shape of a cross or a + **formation**. Jesus put any human effort to contribute to our eternal salvation to death! This is no coincidence that Jesus died on a structure that carries the resemblance of a plus mathematical sign (+). It is a constant reminder to us all that any human ingenuity that wants to add on to what Jesus did for our salvation is simply futile and inferior to what Jesus accomplished on the cross: *Justification by faith!*

NOTES:

....

....

....

....

....

....

....

....

....

....

THE GARDEN TOMB COULD NOT HIDE OUR **KING**: Genesis 2:8-9/15-17/Genesis 3:1-7/13/24 with John 19:38-20:18

INTRODUCTION:

If the body of Jesus received proper burial late Friday afternoon, why did women visit his tomb early Sunday morning? The Gospels tell that the women brought spices with them (Mark 16:1; Luke 24:1). They did this because of the Jewish custom of visiting the tomb of the recently deceased every day for one week (Josephus, *Ant.* 17.200; *Semahot* 12.1; cf. Gen 50:10; 1 Sam 31:13). This was primary burial, or the first funeral, as it were. The spices and perfume helped mask the unpleasant odour of the decomposing corpse. One year later, as prescribed by Jewish custom (*b. Qiddushin* 31b), family members gathered up the skeletal remains and placed them in a niche, or in an ossuary (*m. Sanh.* 6:6; *Semahot* 12.9). In the case of one executed, the remains were collected from the burial place of shame and placed in the family tomb or other place of honour (*m. Sanh.* 6:5–6; *Semahot* 13.7). The belief was that after one year of death, and the consequent wasting away of the flesh, removed the stain of guilt.

CONTENT:

As it turns out, all of their preparations and plans were thrown to the wind. When they arrive at the place of burial, they found that the stone has been rolled aside and there is no body of Jesus to be anointed. There will be no one week of private, quiet mourning. What has happened? It is probable that they assumed that the body of Jesus had been removed by the Jewish authorities, perhaps on the grounds that the body should have been placed in a tomb previously used and designated for the burial of the executed. Perhaps, the kindness of Joseph of Arimathea in making his not-yet-used tomb available for Jesus had been over ridden by the high priest. It is not likely that the first thing that popped into the minds of the women was resurrection.

Question: *Why would the Gospel of John specifically remind us that Jesus was buried in a Garden? Why would Jesus make his first appearance after his resurrection, in a garden?*

I do believe that the answer lies exactly in the context of the *Garden*:

What Adam and Eve had lost in the Garden of Eden to Satan...Jesus had regained in the Garden tomb. Just put differently: What was lost to us in the Garden of Eden was regained for us by Jesus in the Garden tomb:

- We lost in the Garden of Eden an intimate relationship with God...Jesus regained it for us (John 20:17).
- We lost in the Garden of Eden the privilege of eternal Life with God...Jesus regained it for us (John 20:31).

CLOSING:

The resurrection of Jesus in a garden is therefore not a coincidence! The location was chosen by God to make two profound statements:

First: What was taken from us in the Garden of Eden, by the scheme of Satan, was fully regained by the sacrificial death and resurrection of Jesus. Jesus appearance to Mary Magdalene (John 20:14) as his first appearance to humanity, after his resurrection, was a proclamation of *restoration*.

Second: The theme of the Bible is one of *Restoration*! Easter is the ultimate story of God restoring creation back to us and ultimately to Himself.

NOTES:

....

....

....

....

....

....

....

....

....

....

LOOK UPWARDS FOR YOUR SALVATION IS NEAR: Numbers 21:4-9/John 3:14-15

INTRODUCTION:

We see the righteous judgment God brought upon Israel for murmuring, from these scriptures. God sent fiery serpents among them, which bit or stung many to death. Finally, they would turn to God for healing and recovery. Israel's mistrusting of God, amidst many wonders and miracles that he performed to their advantage in the wilderness, came at a huge cost.

The Hebrew term translated: "bronze" can also mean "copper". The area through which the Israelites were traveling in the dessert had copper mines, and archaeologists have found a 5 inch long (13 cm) copper snake in an ancient worship area in a Midianite shrine at Timna. The redness of copper suggested atonement...as does many references in the Old Testament.

CONTENT:

God made a wonderful provision for their relief and rescue. Jewish rabbis and scholars say it was not the sight of the brazen serpent that cured; *but in looking up to it.* Israel looked up to God as the Lord that heals. Our Saviour declared in *John 3:14-15* that as Moses lifted up the serpent in the wilderness, so the Son of man must be lifted up, that whatsoever believeth in him, should not perish.

They looked and lived, and we, if we believe, shall not perish. It is by faith that *we look unto Jesus, Hebrews 12:2... "fixing our eyes on Jesus"...* to look away from your immediate surroundings. Whosoever looked, however desperate his case, or feeble his sight, or distant his place, was certainly and perfectly cured:

- *Do not look downwards.* If the Israelites looked downwards they would have seen the snakes operating in bringing death to everyone in their path. They would have seen only despair and death among themselves. Do not look downwards towards the earth for the world cannot save you or me from eternal death (Luke 21:25-28).
- *Do not look towards those next to you.* I cannot save you and you cannot save me. We can at the most pray for one another (Numbers 21:7) but man cannot bring forth righteousness among each other.
- *Do not look towards yourself for salvation and a solution.* For every one of us are suffering from the death-carrying venom that the Bible calls sin that runs through our whole being (Rom. 7:19-20, 24-25).
- *LOOK UPWARDS...look towards the cross on Golgotha... look towards Jesus who is your salvation!*

CLOSING:

When a boat finds itself in stormy waters there is no sense in leaving the anchor on deck...the anchor needs to be thrown out into the deep ocean to anchor the boat. Our salvation is never secured in our self. The Rock that we need to anchor our faith to is outside of ourselves....in Jesus Christ. Lift up your head and look towards the cross.

NOTES:

....

....

....

....

....

....

....

....

....

....

MOVING INTO THE PURPOSE OF GOD – Ezekiel 47:1-12/John 7:38-39

INTRODUCTION:

Question: What do most people have in common when it comes to improving our lives? *CHANGE*...we want to see positive change! In our work, health, finances, politics, nation...etc.

Ezekiel was a prophet-priest that lived and worked in the Jewish community of exiled Judeans in Babylon. These people have literally lost everything: there homes and belongings to be enslaved under a foreign government in a foreign country. Therefore it is meaningful that the name: Ezekiel means "*God strengthens.*" Ezekiel's ministry was therefore not only to help these Judeans understand that it was due to their own sinful disobedience that they were in bondage, but also to encourage them that God would bring an outcome in spite of their desperate situation.

This happened in a series of visions describing the Jewish temple – *Ezek.40:1-4.* Change was coming to Judah, because God had a plan and purpose for his people, even in spite of their tough context. God's plan of restoration for Israel and Judah would in time be an important link into his salvation strategy for the world.

CONTENT:

It is important to understand some of the descriptive actions and signs in these visions. The *temple*, as described in the Old Testament, represents the dwelling place of God. Especially the holy of holies where the Ark of the Covenant was kept (*Psalm 132:13-14).* The water was initially coming from underneath the door that was the entrance into the inner court (temple). This *doorway* represents Jesus the son of God (*John 10:9*). The *water flowing from the temple* represents the Holy Spirit *(John 7:38-39). Moving water* represents Life just as stagnant water represents death.

God the Father, the Son and the Holy Spirit (The trinity) had a purpose for Israel and Judah and that was that once the Holy Spirit was released on the day of Pentecost (on those that were at the temple for the spring harvest festivity), the Gospel (Good News) of Jesus Christ would spread from the Jewish nation (*represented by the Temple*) to reach all nations even unto the ends of the world *(Acts 1:6-8).*

Water (Holy Spirit) flows ankle deep.........Jerusalem (local community).

Water (Holy Spirit) flows knee deep..........Judea (Province).

Water (Holy Spirit) flows waist deep.........Samaria (Country).

Water (Holy Spirit) flows river deep..........World.

CLOSING:

What will happen as the Holy Spirit restore new life into our community and world?

- The impossible will become possible (Living creatures in the salty Dead Sea – 47:8-9).
- Provision and abundance will follow on lack and need (47:10-12).
- Healing will happen in those places where depression and death exists (47:12).

The Change that the Spirit will bring through the Gospel of Christ will result in life and purpose!

NOTES:

....

....

....

....

....

....

....

....

....

....

NO GUTS....NO GLORY –
Matthew.16:24 - 17:13

INTRODUCTION:

As Jesus physical suffering and death was drawing near Jesus called Peter, James and John- the brother of James- to travel with him to a mountain for prayer. As they were attending to this the transfiguration of Jesus took place as God the Father was revealing His Glory to Jesus as an encouragement to Jesus for the suffering that was upon Him.

CONTENT:

In this moment of transfiguration *Moses* and *Elijah* appeared to Jesus to encourage him and support him in knowing that Jesus sacrificial death was near. Moses who was instrumental in rescuing Israel from Egyptian bondage was encouraging Jesus on his way to soon be freeing all of humanity from the bondage of sin. Elijah who was one of the greatest prophets in Israel's history, was known for challenging the bad kings for not living in accordance with God's covenant and because of that almost always had his life threatened. Knowing that Jesus challenged the Pharisees ungodly ministries and because of that endured constant conflict with the Jewish religious leaders, Elijah encourage Jesus knowing that the authorities will soon capture Him.

So, picture this if you can! Moses being the representative of the *LAW*. Elijah representing the *PROPHETS* of Israel and Jesus representing the Perfect *PRIEST.* One will never get closer to the *GLORY OF GOD* than this. For any Jew this is as good as it gets! This is to be in the presence of God and to experience the glory of God! It is such a great experience to be in the presence of God with like-minded men. *You feel like staying there and capturing that heavenly anointing forever!*

This is exactly what is going on in Peters mind (17:4). Let's hang on to the glory of God as long as possible. Let's not lose this.....lets built a building to be able to capture the glory of God. As soon as Peter starts gathering building material, the glory of God is lost... instantly!

Peter is so short of memory for just a week earlier, Jesus spoke to his disciples on the important topic of taking up your cross. The cross always precede the glory. Jesus is about to enter suffering and death and only once he carried his cross to die on it......the glory of God would be revealed.

We can't share in the glory of Christ unless we are willing to share in the responsibility to be a disciple, taking up our cross daily.

CLOSING:

We can find ourselves so focused on experiencing the glory of God that we can lose perspective on what the church is all about:

WE ARE NOT CALLED TO "GO UP" INTO THE GLORY OF GOD, BUT FOR THE GLORY OF GOD- TO GO OUT INTO THE WORLD!

Acts 1:6-8.

6 "Then they gathered around him and asked him, "Lord, are you at this time going to restore the kingdom to Israel?"

7 He said to them: "It is not for you to know the times or dates the Father has set by his own authority. 8 But you will receive power when the Holy Spirit comes on you; and you will be my witnesses in Jerusalem, and in all Judea and Samaria, and to the ends of the earth."

The disciples were asking: "Lord when will you reveal your glory among your people?" Jesus answered: "That is not what you should be focusing on (you have it all wrong) you need to take your cross and follow me into the world!"

NOTES:

....

....

....

....

....

....

....

....

....

....

GIVE ME **OIL** IN MY LAMP… KEEP ME BURNING. Leveticus.6:8-13/Acts 2:1-4

INTRODUCTION:

Three separate piles of wood burned atop the burning altar. The largest of these was where all the portions of the sacrifices were burned in accordance with the sin offering (this represents the Christians call to daily confession). The second fire provided the coals for the Altar of Incense within the sanctuary (this represents the Christian call to daily prayer), and the third was the "*perpetual fire*" which constantly burned on the altar. Nothing was placed on it, and no coals were taken from it. It existed solely to full fill the commandment that there be a perpetual fire, as the Torah states: "*And a fire shall burn there on the altar constantly; it shall not be extinguished" (Leviticus 6:12-13).* This third fire represents the Christian calling to serve and minister. It was this fire that reminded Israel that they are a chosen race and that God have a special calling on their lives! Moses saw a burning bush alight with fire, but without burning up…at this burning bush he received his calling (Ex.3:1-4).

There was no commandment regarding the type of wood to be used; however, the Rabbis forbade the use of olive wood and grape vine, as these would not burn well and needed to be conserved because of their commercial value to the people. Three particular types of wood were preferred: fig, walnut, and pine. These woods all burn well, and were therefore preferable. The choicest branches of fig were used for the second fire, the one from which coals were taken for the Altar of Incense. If all of the lamps of the menorah went out, they would have to be rekindled from the fire on the Altar of Burnt Offering.

CONTENT:

Moses had a calling for his own people to see them being set free from Egyptian slavery. As he tried to pursue his calling and put into practice what he thought was from God, it went horrible wrong when Moses killed an Egyptian and had to flee from Egypt to Midian. Attending for forty years to sheep in the dessert Moses consciously forgotten about Gods calling on his life....until that day he was reminded at the burning bush that would not die, that God had not forgotten.

The priests in the tabernacle or temple worked in shifts. There were day and night shifts. When the day shift priests arrived for temple service those attending to the altar cleaned out the altar except for the perpetual fire. In the early morning around dusk when the new shift of priest arrived they would find the fire almost completely burned out just in time to get it going again. They would simply put wood on the coals, take a deep breath and *BLOW* to see the fire start again.

Acts 2:1-4.

"When the day of Pentecost came, they were all together in one place.
2 Suddenly a sound like the blowing of a violent wind came from heaven and filled the whole house where they were sitting. 3 They saw what seemed to be tongues of fire that separated and came to rest on each of them. 4 All of them were filled with the Holy Spirit and began to speak in other tongues as the Spirit enabled them."

On the day of Pentecost we find a re-enactment of what those altar priest did every day: Igniting the calling of God in the life of the Apostles. There came a *PNOE/WIND ("Breath" in Hebrew)* that ignited Gods calling in their Lives. The Holy Spirit blew the calling of God on the Apostles into being! The Holy Spirit is the breath of

God that was send to ignite His calling on your life every time you choose to forget about it, to neglect it or to let it go to waste!

CLOSING:

In 2 Tim. 1:6-9, Paul commands Timothy "to rekindle his fire." He uses the Greek word: *Anazōpureo* which translates to: 'keep your calling alive'.

*[6] "For this reason I remind you to **fan into flame** the gift of God, which is in you through the laying on of my hands. [7] For the Spirit God gave us does not make us timid, but gives us power, love and self-discipline. [8] So do not be ashamed of the testimony about our Lord or of me his prisoner. Rather, join with me in suffering for the gospel, by the power of God. [9] He has saved us and called us to a holy life—not because of anything we have done but because of his own purpose and grace. This grace was given us in Christ Jesus before the beginning of time."*

NOTES:

....

....

....

....

....

....

....

....

....

....

POWER IN PRAISE – 2 Chronicles 20:1-30

INTRODUCTION:

In the Old Near East, tribes and nations that were under the rule of a foreign king were always looking out for opportunities to overthrow the oppressing kingdom and government. When the ruling king became old and weary, it was normally a time that oppressed nations wanted to start a rebellion to over throw the ruling party. This is what happened on the eastern border of Judah when Jehoshaphat received the news of a coming attack.

In our lives we experience from time to time that we are up and against circumstances that totally outweigh our capacity to fight it. We are surrounded by circumstances that are simply outnumbering us and leaving us without possibilities. This is such a place and situation that Jehoshaphat found himself in!

Fortunately Jehoshaphat showed wisdom to not rely on his experience or expertise, but fleeing to God and seeking His face! He proclaimed a fast for all of Judah and in this process a Godly word was given as a word instructing the king what to do.

CONTENT:

What was supposed to be a clash of the clans became a worship service (v.20-23):

"Early in the morning they left for the Desert of Tekoa. As they set out, Jehoshaphat stood and said, "Listen to me, Judah and people of Jerusalem! Have faith in the LORD YOUR GOD AND YOU WILL BE UPHELD; HAVE FAITH IN HIS PROPHETS AND YOU WILL BE SUCCESSFUL." [21] *After consulting the people, Jehoshaphat appointed men to sing to the LORD* AND TO PRAISE HIM FOR THE *splendour of his holiness as they went out at the head of the army, saying:*

"Give thanks to the LORD,
for his love endures forever."

[2]*As they began to sing and praise, the Lord* set Ambushes against the men of Ammon and Moab and Mount *Seir who were invading Judah, and they were defeated.* [23] *The Ammonites and Moabites rose up against the men from Mount Seir* to destroy and annihilate them. After they finished slaughtering the men from *Seir, they helped to destroy one another."*

When we face challenges in Life God does not allow us to be passive and ignorant of it as if it is not out there. Israel had to take action! But they were not to follow their own plans but God's. They were to tackle the challenge in facing their circumstances head on, but not with spears and swords, but with prayer and praise. So, God instructs Jehoshaphat to place the church band (worship team) in the front line of fire and the rest of the prayer warriors to follow behind! As Judah started praising God, havoc broke loose as Judah's enemies started killing each other! *When we praise God in song and prayer in spite of our circumstances and challenges God brings about a Godly outcome for us!*

Praising God changes our circumstances from being defeated to being blessed (v.24-26).

[24] *"When the men of Judah came to the place that overlooks the desert and looked toward the vast army, they saw only dead bodies lying on*

the ground; no one had escaped. [25] *So, Jehoshaphat and his men went to carry off their plunder, and they found among them a great amount of equipment and clothingand also articles of value—more than they could take away. There was so much plunder that it took three days to collect it.* [26] *On the fourth day they assembled in the Valley of Berakah, where they praised the LORD. This is why it is called the Valley of Berakah* to this day."

Israel's enemies wanted to bring defeat onto Israel and ruin them, but God changed all of that to a blessing! The Valley of death became the valley of blessing....*Berakah* means blessing! (*Deriving from the word: Baruk = praise*). When we commit ourselves to *Baruk* (praise) it enables us to focus not on our circumstances but on God, which is greater than any challenges we need to face.

Praise is powerful, because it is an offering of thanksgiving to God (v.27-28).

[27] "*Then, led by Jehoshaphat, all the men of Judah and Jerusalem returned joyfully to Jerusalem, for the LORD* had given them cause to rejoice over their enemies. [28] *They entered Jerusalem and went to the temple of the LORD* with harps and lyres and trumpets."

It is interesting that on the return of the men from the Valley of blessing, they go straight to the temple to give thanks to God. They not only go to the temple to present the bait to God, but especially to continue giving thanks to Him for their rescue and protection. They learned that day that their true wealth were not their material gain, but Yahweh, the God of Israel.

CLOSING:

Why do we need to respect and support our praise and worship team (musicians)?

- They help us focus on God and not our problems (v.12c).
- They lead us onto spiritual victory (v.15b).
- They lead us into the Lord's blessing (v.26).

NOTES:

....

....

....

....

....

....

....

....

....

....

GOD's **QUALITY** BUILDING PROGRAM IS HIS PEOPLE SURRENDERING TO THE HOLY SPIRIT - Zechariah 4

INTRODUCTION:

Zechariah was a priest and therefore a member of a priestly family who returned from Babylon with Zerubbabel in about 538 BC. Zechariah finds the people of Israel being discourage as the rebuilding of their community and temple did not happen as planned. The foundation of the temple had been laid shortly after the initial return, in 536 BC. But powerful opposition had prevented any further progress on rebuilding the temple. There was little evidence of the kind of transformation of the state of things that the earlier prophets had anticipated, whether externally in a restoration of Jewish sovereignty or internally in a moral reformation of the people. So, Zechariah was called to encourage his people to start a fresh with rebuilding their lives and especially the temple.

CONTENT:

The angel of the Lord focuses Zechariah's attention on the *Lampstand of Gold.* This reminds him of the menorah in the Tabernacle or temple of old and is for us a symbol of the church (Rev.1:12/20). Therefore, giving a hint to the reader that the issue at hand has to do with how we must go about (re)building our community of faith for God's glory.

Principle 1: Zechariah 4:6

"This is the word of the Lord to Zerubbabel: 'Not by might nor by power, but by my Spirit,' says the L*ORD Almighty."*

The best decision to make when focussing on building anew our community of believers, our church…is to surrender completely to the person and power of the Holy Spirit. It is not by our strength that the mountains in our way are demolished but through the intervention of the Spirit. It is not by our might that the pathways are cleared before us of obstacles, but only through the Divinity of the Holy Spirit.

Principle 2: Zechariah 4:9-10

9 *"The hands of Zerubbabel have laid the foundation of this temple; his hands will also complete it. Then you will know that the Lord* Almighty *has sent me to you.*

10 *"Who dares despise the day of small things, since the seven eyes of the* LORD that range throughout the earth will rejoice *when they see the chosen capstone in the hand of Zerubbabel?"*

We are warned to not despise the small breakthroughs when building and investing in our community of believers. We need to focus at first on the small breakthroughs that God accomplishes in the life of our church ministries as this will build our faith to trust God for the big miracles to come! *IF WE WANT TO SEE THE BIG BREAKTHROUGHS IN OUR CHURCHES, WE FIRST NEED TO START THANKING GOD FOR THE SMALL MIRACLES IN OUR MINISTRIES!* Need I remind you of the miracle that took place when Jesus had to feed the multitudes? It was a boy giving his lunch box to Jesus of fish and bread. When Jesus started thanking God for this small obedience from a child, the miracle and breakthrough came when the multitudes were fed from the content of this same lunch box!

Principle 3: Zechariah 4:12-14

"Again I asked him, "What are these two olive branches beside the two gold pipes that pour out golden oil?"

[13] He replied, "Do you not know what these are?"

"No, my lord," I said.

[14] So he said, "These are the two who are anointed to serve the Lord of all the earth."

God always builds his church through PEOPLE - through *US! YOU and ME.* People with a servant heart and a sense of calling. The two branches of the olive tree represents Zerubbabel the governor and Jesua the high priest. Gods anointed are the living 'stones' that he uses to build his church:

[5] you also, like living stones, are being built into a spiritual house to be a holy priesthood, offering spiritual sacrifices acceptable to God through Jesus Christ (1 Peter 2:5).

People are key to God's strategy of reaching the community and the world with the hope of the Holy Spirit.

CLOSING:

The anointing that God use to bless our initiative in building his church, his people and his Kingdom are:

- Faith to trust the Holy Spirit and not our human engineering.
- Gratitude to thank God for the smallest miracle and for humble beginnings.
- A Willingness to make oneself available for God and his call.

NOTES:

....

....

....

REVELATION of the Father heart of God! – 2 Kings 6:1-7

INTRODUCTION:

In 2 Kings 2 we are told that Elijah was taken up into heaven by a chariot of fire. Before taking of he blessed Elisha, his intern and junior, with a double portion of his anointing. Instantly we see Elisha performing supernatural acts as part of his prophetic ministry.

The school of the prophets, here spoken of, seems to be the one at Gilgal, for there Elisha was (4:38) and it was near Jordan; and probably wherever Elisha resided as many as could of the sons of the prophets flocked to him for the advantage of his instructions, counsels, and prayers. Everyone would covet to dwell with him and be near him. Their number increased so that they wanted room.

God's prophets have seldom been the world's favourites. So poor were they that they could not hire workmen (but must leave their studies, and work for themselves) and had no tools, but must borrow of their neighbours. Poverty then is no bar to prophecy. However, they were industrious men, and willing to take pains.

CONTENT:

"Oh no"...he cried out... "It was borrowed"...when the iron axe head fell into the water!

This poor prophet had no money to repay the borrower for the lost axe head, but was under the Law of Moses to do so:

Exodus 22:14 *"If anyone borrows an animal from their neighbour and it is injured or dies while the owner is not present, they must make restitution."*

Proverbs 22:7 *"The rich rule over the poor, and the borrower is slave to the lender."*

Elisha who was himself a prophet and poor understood the predicament that his colleague was under and came to the specific prophet's rescue. Put aside the miracle, Elisha as the prophet of God saw an opportunity to reveal to all the bystanders that the God of Israel has compassion as well as a heart for the poor and those in financial despair. Therefore, it is important to understand that prophets' primary calling is not to prophesy on Gods behalf or to do miracles, *BUT TO REVEAL THE HEART AND CHARACTER OF GOD!*

Many understand prophecy to be primarily speaking and acting on Gods behalf. When in actual fact it is closer to the truth that a prophet is to know and reveal the heart of God. The prophet is to SHOW us who God is! Elisha knew God's passionate heart for one that is caught up in debt and have no way to repay it and revealed Gods heart by rescuing the axe from the lake. This incident reveals to us that God wants to come to our aid when we are drowning under financial debt and hardship.

CLOSING:

On the flip side of the same coin, we can find ourselves hitting rock bottom – in to deep- when it comes to sin. We may be drowning… sinking and being pulled further down into the deep by the gravity of sin. This prophet's dilemma was a heavy axe head sinking to the bottom of a lake. Others suffer because of a heavy heart sinking into a deep pit of despair.

Col.2:13-14 says: "God made you alive with Christ. He forgave us all our sins[14] having cancelled the charge of our legal indebtedness, which stood against us and condemned us; he has taken it away, nailing it to the cross." Blotting out the handwriting of ordinances that was against us.

What Elisha did for his colleague, Jesus did for us on the cross. It is finished -the outstanding account has been paid in full.

NOTES:

....

....

....

....

....

....

....

....

....

....

BY MY **SPIRIT**... Celebrating Pentecost, Acts 2:1-14/36-41 and Ephesians 1:1-14

INTRODUCTION:

Question: What was the social and religious context in Acts 2?

On Shavuot (The festival of weeks), the Israelites brought an offering of the first crops of spring to the Tabernacle and later, to the Temple in Jerusalem to celebrate the first of the harvest. It is a time when God commands his people to give a freewill offering. The people were to bring something, giving in proportion to how he has blessed them: *"No one should appear before the LORD empty-handed: Each of you must bring a gift in proportion to the way the LORD your God has blessed you. (Deuteronomy 16:16–17)"*

When each family presented its basket to the Lord before the *Kohen* (Priest), they recited the following:[15]

"My father was a wandering Aramean, and he went down into Egypt with a few people and lived there and became a great nation, powerful and numerous. But the Egyptians mistreated us and made us suffer, subjecting us to harsh labour."

[15] eTeacher Biblical – Israel Academy of Language and History

"Then we cried out to the Lord, the God of our ancestors, and the Lord heard our voice and saw our misery, toil, and oppression. So the Lord brought us out of Egypt with a mighty hand and an outstretched arm, with great terror and with signs and wonders. He brought us to this place and gave us this land, a land flowing with milk and honey; and now I bring the first fruits of the soil that you, Lord, have given me" (Deuteronomy 26:5–10).

The above explains why there were so many Jews and God-fearing Jews at that time in Jerusalem with the outpouring of the Holy Spirit. These people were gathering from all corners of the known world to celebrate the festival of weeks...bringing to God the first of their crop as a gift of thanks giving for the Promised Land.

CONTENT:

Question: Why would God choose to send the Holy Spirit to convert mankind at the time that it was the festival of the first fruit?

The 3000 that accepted Jesus Christ as Lord and Saviour was only the *BEGINNING* of the heavenly harvest....*only the first of the fruit to come into the Kingdom, because of the gift of the Holy Spirit.* A bigger spiritual harvest was to follow: *Acts 4:4* witness that those that came to faith grew to 5000, *Acts 6:7* confirms that the numbers still increased "rapidly" and *Acts 9:31* teaches that this was an ongoing and occurring event as the gospel message spread.

Question: What is the significance of the gift of the Holy Spirit? – Ephesians 1:13-14

The Holy Spirit has been given to us as a deposit. When you book a holiday and you pay a deposit you are engaging into a legal contract whereby you confirm that you are committed to honour the agreement and that you will pay the outstanding amount of money by the due date.

When you want to buy a house or a car you pay a deposit as you are engaging into a legal contract whereby you confirm that you are committed to honour the agreement and that you will pay the outstanding amount of money by the due date.

By sending the Holy Spirit God is entering into a binding contract with us in making it known that he is giving the deposit (Holy Spirit) as a guarantee that He will keep to His promise and commitment of giving us our full inheritance –eternal life in His Kingdom. The significance of the gift of the Holy Spirit is that God will keep to all his promises!

CLOSING:

We have seen that the Holy Spirit is the "first fruit" (just the beginning) of God's future promises for his Church – his people.

Prayer:

As we go now to our daily living…

May the Spirit come to us in new and exciting ways.

As a gentle whisper, in dreams, in silence, in prayer.

As a strong wind, in lives filled with love and compassion;

As a mighty storm, in exuberant hearts of joy.

So let us go now, filled with the Spirit all our days.

NOTES:

....

....

....

....

....

....

....

BECAUSE HE LIVES I CAN FACE **TOMORROW** – John 20:1-10

INTRODUCTION:

The gospel of John uses symbols extensively to assist the reader to connect with the fascinating story of Jesus to reveal that He is truly the sent one from God. For instance, John 2:1-12 uses the symbol of *water* changed into *wine* to reveal that through the intervention of Christ *temporarily* life changes into *eternal* life! The result of John using signs as a means of communication is to help unbelievers become believers (2:11).

CONTENT:

"Early on the first day of the week, while it was still dark, Mary
Magdalene went to the tomb and saw that the stone had been removed
from the entrance. 2 So she came running to Simon Peter and the other
disciple, the one Jesus loved, and said, "They have taken the Lord out of
the tomb, and we don't know where they have put him!"

3 So Peter and the other disciple started for the tomb. 4 Both were running,
but the other disciple out ran Peter and reached the tomb first. 5 He bent
over and looked in at the strips of linen lying there but did not go in. 6
Then Simon Peter came along behind him and went straight into the

tomb. He saw the strips of linen lying there, [7] as well as the cloth that had been wrapped around Jesus' head. The cloth was still lying in its place, separate from the linen. [8] Finally the other disciple, who had reached the tomb first, also went inside. He saw and believed. [9] (They still did not understand from Scripture that Jesus had to rise from the dead.) [10] Then the disciples went back to where they were staying."

The above reading needs some cultural clarification for the purpose of this interpretation:

Among the rich in the Old Near East, household slaves would serve the meal. When the meal was finished the father of the household will place the table cloth that is in use, rolled up on the table as a sign to the slave that the meal was finished and that he can clear the table.

If the meal was interrupted for some reason or other and the family or father had to attend to something before they or he could again attend to the food, he would place the table cloth wrapped neatly on the table. In doing this he was giving an intentional sign to the slave that the meal is not finished for he will return to attend to the meal again.

The head cloth that Jesus wore were *wrapped* or folded up (*entulissoo* in New Testament Greek), meaning to be a signal to those that would enter the grave that he (Jesus) was not done...he would soon return to have fellowship with his disciples!

CLOSING:

With the resurrection of Jesus we see indeed this sign that was left in his grave, come to fulfilment in Jesus appearance to his disciples, but also his future return to make all things new:

- John 20:11-14: Jesus appearing to Mary Magdalene.
- John 20:19-22: Jesus returning to his disciples for the first time.
- John 20:24-28: Jesus returning to his disciples for a second time.
- John 21:1-25: Jesus returning to his disciples for a third time.

- ACTS 1:9-11. Jesus will return for he promised to gather His church for a heavenly meal in the house of his Father.

NOTES:

....

....

....

....

....

....

....

....

....

....

UNQUALIFIED? – Judges 6:1-39

INTRODUCTION:

In the time of the Judges Israel had settled into Canaan and divided the land into 11 regions for each tribe (except for the tribe of Levi). The tribes separated from each other as they were now attending to their own tribal community life. On the downside there was now not any centralised leadership as was the case when Moses or Joshua took charge of Israel. Each tribe had their own local leadership. Unfortunately…..not having a centralised leadership anymore led to two critical scenarios:

- Some tribes neglecting the worship of Yahweh, fell into idol worship.
- The Philistines knowing that Israel was not as unified as before, used this as an opportunity to drive them out of Canaan.

In a critical time as this, God raised up judges or informal leaders to rescue his people from total despair and disaster.

CONTENT:

GOD SEE/EXPERIENCE US IN AN DIFFERENT LIGHT THAN WE SEE OURSELVES (v.12).

God focuses on our potential! It is quite ironic: Gideon is hiding from the Philistine's feeling defeated and belittled, but in spite of all of this God sends His angel addressing Gideon as: MIGHTY WARRIOR! God saw Gideon's potential and taped into that. Gideon saw himself as a farmer just getting by….God saw him as an INFORMAL LEADER TAKING HIS TRIBE INTO BATTLE! There is so much more to us if only we could see ourselves through the eyes of God!

GOD IS NOT SEARCHING FOR SUPER HUMAN BEINGS, BUT PEOPLE THAT ARE WILLING TO BE USED BY HIM IN SUPER NATURAL WAYS (v.14).

There is no limit to what God can do. There is also no limit to what God can do through us if we allow Him access to our lives. God is not expecting from us to supply and produce what we do not have, but only to be obedient in the strength and resources that we do have. What is necessary though and what is important for us, is to have God's authority to move in his name and power. With his backing and support we already know what the outcome will be like!

*GOD DOES NOT EXCLUSIVELY USE THE INFLUENTIAL, BUT HE OFTEN USES THE UNEXPECTED and the UNQUALIFIED ONES! (v.15)***.** God used a downtown teenage girl to give birth - and raise the Saviour of the world! Jesus called fishermen and tax collectors to become His disciples and future apostles of the Good News! Church history – and secular history is filled with evidence of God using humanity in obedience to him to create the impossible and bring about what is incomprehensible.

WE NEVER FAIL GOD IN REGARDS TO WHO WE ARE, WHERE WE COME FROM OR OUR FAMILY'S BACKGROUND…WE EITHER EXHALT OR FAIL GOD ON BEING OBEDIENT TO HIS CALL OR NOT! (v.25-26). God will most likely prepare you for informal and spontaneous leadership by first teaching you and testing you on familiar ground before sending you off into more hostile territory. Gideon first had to destroy the idols of his father on familiar land, before God allowed him to destroy the philistine's armies on hostile ground. GOD JUST LOVES GROWING AND

GROOMING ORDINARY PEOPLE INTO DOING THE EXTRA-ORDINARY.

GODLY LEADERSHIP HAS LESS TO DO WITH POSITION, OR QUALIFICATION. IT HAS TO DO WITH THE ANOINTING OF GOD. THE SPIRIT OF GOD EMPOWERS US AS ORDINARY PEOPLE TO PERFORM DEEDS AND LEADERSHIP ACTS OF THE EXTRA-ORDINARY (v. 34-35). We find a completely different Gideon in verse 34 than in verse 12. In verse 12 Gideon was a farmer with farming implements in his hand. In verse 34 Gideon is taking on the role of a warrior blowing on the shofar (taking on the role of a soldier). God does not only perceive us from a different perspective, he also transforms us to fit into our true calling and potential.

CLOSING:

In today's top notch society it is unexpected to have unqualified people step into a profession without proper training or education. When it comes to the Kingdom of God and spiritual principles we find other criteria come into play. Discipleship can best be described as an internship where we become qualified as we proceed to the following level and accomplish what is set out in front of us. In this kind of internship is it best to remember that God qualifies us as we trust and obey.

NOTES:

....

....

....

....

....

....

THE VALUE OF TIME – Exodus 13:17-22

INTRODUCTION:

When Moses took the Israelites out of Egypt he could have made it to Canaan in a little more than one week. Instead he took them on a route that began a 40 year journey. This is to completely freak out those you and I know who are highly organised and consciously working at improving their time management skills! In Moses defence it has to be said that he did not choose this route, because he was confused or lost. He was guided by God for specific reasons:

CONTENT:

The shorter route would have taken Israel through hostile Philistine country:

When Israel left Egypt they were mostly broken souls who spent the last generations as slaves who were in no condition, at that time, to undertake such a confrontational challenge. They were not prepared for such hostility. God sometimes need to bring us along the "*detour*" because we are mentally, emotionally and spiritually, unprepared to face what awaits us.

GOD TAKES US ON THE LONGER ROUTE TO PROTECT US FOR OUR OWN WELLBEING.

God took Israel on the longer route because He needed to give them time to get to know Him:

In the wilderness the people of Israel would have had an opportunity to meditate on and encounter God (YHWH) in ways they could not on the shorter route. This was the time God needed to reveal to Israel their future and Gods plan for them. Consider the miraculous crossing of the red sea, provision of water, manna and Quail.

GOD TAKES US ON THE LONGER ROUTE TO GROW US.

God took Israel on the longer route because He needed to prepare them for what was coming:

The wilderness born Israelites knew nothing of slavery. They did not have a victim mentality or idealized slavery like their parents use to do when they got scared or tired on their wilderness journey. They grew up to become an army of seasoned warriors ready to take on the promised land…to do whatever it takes to step into their Godly inheritance. To do that they would have to fight many battles against strange enemy tribes and on territory they did not know.

GOD TAKES US ON THE LONGER ROUTE TO PREPARE US.

CLOSING:

What to do while God is setting me up for the longer route?

- Don't fight God, He is doing it for your own protection or benefit.
- Read and study the Bible to grow continuously in God and your understanding of God's purpose for your current journey and future life.
- Make time to pray and to discern what God may be preparing you for?

NOTES:

....

....

....

....

....

....

....

....

....

....

WORKING FOR GOD OR WITNESSING GOD AT **WORK?** – Acts 8:26-40

INTRODUCTION:

QUESTION:

Which option do you think works for the best? WORKING FOR GOD or WITNESSING GOD AT WORK? Which one of these two options will outlast the other?

Ethiopia was a kingdom since 750 B.C. The country back then was ruled by women and the ruling queens had the title of *Kandake.* Because women ruled this country all men that were in the queen's service had to be emasculated to ensure that the queen would not be raped. So how did it happen that one of these male officials, a eunuch, came to Jerusalem in seeking his salvation in Judaism?

On the border of Egypt and Ethiopia was a small established community of Jews who reached out to the people of Ethiopia in searching for proselytes (people to convert from heathenism to the Jewish faith). Most probably this eunuch was influenced by the proselyting Jewish group on his country's border and wanted to visit Jerusalem to investigate further into the religion of Judaism or go worship YHWEH as a *God fearer.*

Now look at the evidence as we study the conversion story of the eunuch. The Holy Spirit is the **active agent** and Philip in ministering to the eunuch continuously takes on a passive role! This is a powerful story of simply experiencing *God at work.*

CONTENT:

THE HOLY SPIRIT PREPARED OR PROVIDED....

- The Road/location (v.26).
- The Scripture: Isaiah 53: 7-8 (v. 28/ 32-33).
- The "address" (v.29).
- The invitation coming from the eunuch to sit with him (v. 31).
- The teachable spirit of the eunuch that was longing for answers (v. 34).
- The water for baptism (v.36).
- Philip's next missionary appointment (v.40).

When we read the book of Acts it is really not so much the Acts of the Apostles as it is the acts of the Holy Spirit directing and timing the work of God!

CLOSING:

The acts of the Apostle Philip, describe the baptism of this Ethiopian eunuch shortly after the death of Christ. Eusebius of Caesarea, the first church historian, in his "*Ecclesiastical History*" further tells of how the eunuch returned to Ethiopia to share the Christian teachings in his native land shortly after the resurrection and prior to the arrival of the Apostle Matthew.

Before the Ethiopian king Ezana (whose kingdom was then called Aksum) embraced Christianity for himself and decreed it for his kingdom (c. 330 A.D.), his nation had already constituted a large number of Christians thanks to the pioneering work of the God – fearer eunuch who was converted by the Holy Spirit to Christianity. This Eunuch took Christianity back to his own people and country making it most probably the first Christian nation!

Working for God is never in vain and should never be discouraged. But witnessing and seeing God at work is priceless! It does not only result in a Godly outcome, but also pay Godly dividends long after the actual event.

NOTES:

....

....

....

....

....

....

....

....

....

....

HAVE YOU EVER LOST YOUR **XMAS PRESENT?** - Luke 2:41-52

INTRODUCTION:

Have you ever lost a Christmas gift than was given to you? Maybe jewellery that was given to you by your partner or spouse? Maybe it was a gift card to spend at one or other retailor or even some cash in an envelope? What a difficult situation to find oneself in…not even to mention the guilt and shame!

CONTENT:

The Gospel of Luke (2:41-52) tells us that losing one's Christmas gift is not as rare as we might think. It is exactly what happened to Mary and Joseph-the parents of Jesus! This happened during the time of the Passover celebrations in Jerusalem. Jewish men were required to go to 3 feasts in Jerusalem. Those feasts were Passover (Easter), Pentecost and the Feast of Tabernacles, though only Passover was strictly observed. Luke tells us that Mary and Joseph with Jesus was travelling to Jerusalem to attend Passover. This specific Passover was special, for Jesus would join Joseph and the other men in celebrating in the temple. During a Jewish boy's twelfth year he was prepared for his induction as a full member of the religious community which took place when he was 13 and so Jesus being 12 years old joined Mary and Joseph.

These pilgrims usually travelled in a large party or caravan as it was too dangerous to travel by oneself. On their return Mary and Joseph assumed that Jesus was somewhere in the crowd, among the other teenagers, making their way back home from Jerusalem. In reality they lost Jesus as he was not among the other children, but he remained behind in the temple in Jerusalem. After three days they found him in the temple courts. They lost (for 3 days) the greatest gift entrusted to human mankind-the Son of God! They lost the greatest Christmas present – the Prince of Peace!

Don't be too hard on Josef and Mary and what seems to be 'parental failure.' It is very easy to experience the joy of Christmas and the excitement of the holidays without acknowledging that God's love is the reason for this great time of the year. It is easy to enter Christmas without acknowledging that Jesus obedience to enter our world is the reason to celebrate. It is human nature to enter the Christmas buzz and survive the great food and conversations and not realise that we have enjoyed another festive season without honouring the Son of God as the greatest Gift to us.

In all honesty…the biggest loss is not to lose one's gift or present after Christmas day, but to lose the true perspective on all of Christmas… that God has given His most expensive and valuable gift – His son Jesus Christ:

John 3:16

"For God so loved the world that he gave his one and only Son, that whoever believes in him shall not perish but have eternal life."

CLOSING:

Only once more would it seem as if we have lost Jesus as the greatest Xmas gift of all times, when he was laid away in a grave. Also for three days he could not be found. His disciples were depressed and hope less as they did not realise that, according to the prophets and Jesus teachings, he would face, challenge and conquer death during the duration of three days before he would let himself be "found" by Mary Magdalene in the Tomb Garden. Jesus has risen from the grave so that whoever seeks after him will be able to find him:

Matthew 7:7-8

Ask, Seek, Knock:

"Ask and it will be given to you; seek and you will find; knock and the door will be opened to you. For everyone who asks receives; the one who seeks finds; and to the one who knocks, the door will be opened."

NOTES:

....

....

....

....

....

....

....

....

....

....

FOREVER **YOUNG**: - John 2:1-12

INTRODUCTION:

Is eternal life for real? Simply speculation or a fantasy? According to St. Paul in 1 Corinthians 15:12-19 life after death is not only a reality, but foundational to what Christianity proclaims and beliefs. This believe, in the resurrection of the dead, has been proclaimed by the Church officially in the *Nicene Creed* for centuries: "*We look forward to the resurrection of the dead, and to life in the world to come.*" The Gospels are off course no stranger to this believe and all four gospels do witness to Jesus being victorious over death.

CONTENT:

A key word in understanding John 2:1-12 is the use of the word *"signs"* in John 2:11. A sign is a reference to something of much greater importance or significance. A notice that says: DANGER – KEEP OUT! Is not only warning against personal injury, but signalling a greater warning in regards to trespassing and the consequences thereof. The word: *semeion* is used in the Greek language for indicating the importance of Biblical *"sign –language"* that wants to fix our attention on a much greater issue.

The sign of water being changed into wine is an event which is regarded as having some special meaning. For instance, in Luke

2:11-12 angels tell shepherds in Bethlehem that they will find a baby wrapped in cloths and lying in a manger. This will be a *sign* to them. A sign of what? *That the expected Messiah has just arrived. That salvation has come.* Why did the wise men from the East so eagerly followed the unusual star that appeared in the eastern skyline? Because it was a *sign* that the King was to be born (Matthew 2:1-2).

What is the sign in John 2 referring to? What is the significance of Jesus turning water into wine? *Water is a sign of temporarily life. Wine is a sign of eternal Life.* Jesus has the power and mandate to turn this life into eternal life…Jesus would be the One that, when he returns as the Bridegroom for the wedding with his church/ bride, will resurrect us for an eternal life with Him (Rev.19:7-9).

This is a sign revealing to us that just as a miracle it is to turn water into wine so Jesus would do this miracle on the cross in transforming this short life on earth into eternal everlasting life with God. The miracle in John 2 is a sign of a greater event that will take place on the cross.

When Jesus side was pierced, according to John 19:33-35, there appeared *blood* and *water. Blood is a sign of our justification* and *water is a sign of our sanctification* which without we cannot enter into eternity with Christ. Through the death of Jesus Christ we became justified (just as if we have not sinned) and sanctified in order to enter into eternity with Christ.

CLOSING:

According to Matthew 27:50-51, the curtain in the temple that separated the holy of hollies and which was reserved for only the high priest (because he was justified and sanctified) now was torn in two. What kept humanity from entering into a relationship with God and spending eternity with Him was now removed, because we too are now sanctified and justified in Christ Jesus.

NOTES:

....

GOD ZONE – Genesis. 12, 13 & 26

INTRODUCTION:

When I for the very first time visited the city of London I made use of the underground public train transport. The very first time I tried to get on to the train it was cramped with people with barely room to move in. An automated voice called out: *"Mind the gap"*...referring to the gap between the platform and the entrance into the train. This voice activated reminder was because of Health & Safety policy. Initially I thought the voice was saying: *"find a gap!"* All considered it could as well have been: "find a gap", because the train was so cramped you had to literally squeeze yourself in among the crowd to find some room on the train before the doors slam shut behind you.

As funny as this story seems this is a serious safety warning for if you do not mind your step and your food get caught up in the space between the platform and the train door you could either be injured or killed if the train took off! *MIND YOUR STEP*...would be the more accurate expression for me!

CONTENT:

In Genesis 12 God promises Abraham that he will bless him on entering- and establishing himself in Canaan. This blessing is not only directed to him, but to those generations to follow. As soon as Abraham does not *mind his step* and crosses the border into another territory-Egypt, the blessing and promises of God is being jeopardized. We sense this when Sarai was taken from Abraham and given to the Egyptian Pharaoh. Sarai is the one that will according to God's divine intervention, give life to Isaac from whose family Jesus would eventually be born (Gen. 21:1-4). But this promise of the Messiah was now severely jeopardized when Abraham did not trust in God's ability to care for them in the midst of famine in Canaan and crossed into a territory where God did not tell him to cross into. Then to make things worse, Abraham lies to the Pharaoh to protect his own life! Graciously God protects both Abraham and Sarai's lives and keeps his hand upon them in the foreign Egyptian country. But the promise of making Abraham into a great nation is at risk! *IF YOU DO NOT MIND YOUR STEP THINGS CAN GET OUT OF HAND!*

As soon as Abraham returns to Canaan (12:20-13:2) and the precise place that he had pitch his tent earlier... (12:8/ 13:3), the land God directed him to, is not only the promise restored of the blessing that will come to all peoples of the earth when the Messiah would be born from the lineage of Isaac, but the overall blessing of God's provision was evident!

The same pattern is to be seen in Genesis 26:1-14. This time the focus is on Isaac! Isaac remained true to God's expectation of Him to mind his step and not cross over to Egypt! Not making the same mistake as his father....well to a certain extend that is!

God's blessing and protection in our lives is not only exclusively based on our obedience, but always on God's faithfulness. This is clear from the above references in Genesis. *BUT WE CAN DELAY THE OUTWORKING OF GOD'S PROMISES IN OUR LIVES IF WE DO NOT MIND OUR STEP! TO UNDERSTAND THIS WE HAVE TO ASK OURSELVES: WHAT HAS GOD ENTRUSTED TO ME/WHAT AM I CARRYING FOR GOD?* Abraham carried the promise of LAND! When he stepped away from what God entrusted to him the outworking of God's promises in his life came into question! When he obediently carried faithfully what God had entrusted to him he was in a perfect relationship with God to witness generational promises coming to pass (Gen.13:10-18).

CLOSING:

What has God entrusted to you? Do you know what you are carrying? If you do, then you can step into it and move in it. Moses carried the responsibility of leadership that is why he could in spite of continuous criticism continue to lead Israel to freedom. Jesus carried the promise of reconciliation (between God and man) that is why he could step into the suffering he had to endure, even unto death. Paul carried the promise of salvation to the gentiles that is how he could in spite of persecution keep on proclaiming the Gospel as an apostle for Jesus. What about you?

NOTES:

....

....

....

....

....

....

....

....

....

....

SERMONS FOR FIXING WHAT IS BROKEN

PREACHING AS PROPHETIC RESPONSIBILITY

WHY **ASCENSION DAY** TOOK PLACE?/ WHY DID JESUS HAD TO LEAVE? – John 5:16-30

INTRODUCTION:

The short answer to the above question is, because Jesus portfolio and responsibility is not only the Church, but all of creation (all aspects of the created universe) he therefore had to leave for his Fathers kingdom from where he is governing what is visible and what is invisible to man (Col. 1:15-17) for unto all eternity.

The extensive answer to our question is partly connected to the Old Testament and partly to the New Testament. The teaching of Jesus in John 5:16-30 is central in all of this and needs to be interpreted against the backdrop of the previous healing miracle that took place on the Sabbath (John 5:1-15).

In Genesis 2:2 God institutes the Sabbath:

> [2] *By the seventh day God had finished the work he had been doing; so on the seventh day he rested from all his work.*

AND

In John 5:17 it seems as if Jesus is overriding what His father instituted as rest in the creation order when He tells the Jewish leaders: *"My Father is always at his work to this very day, and I too am working."*

Jesus healed an invalid on the given Sabbath at the pool of Bethesda and when the Jewish leaders confronted him with the Godly ordination of "resting" on the Sabbath Jesus replied with the response recorded in John 5:17 which seems to be a contradiction in terms with the Genesis account.

CONTENT:

What is Jesus getting at when He says: "My father is always at his work to this very day, and I too am working?"

CURA CONTINUA (God continuously caring for us):

God is done with the creation of the universe and with the ordering and aligning of nature. This becomes clear and evident when the author of the Genesis account repeatedly says that it was *'good'*. But God has not created only too abandon his handy work! Just as the Father created through Jesus the Son…so is the Father constantly caring for all of creation through Jesus His Son. Jesus has therefore rightly returned to the Kingdom of his father to constantly intercede for us in the throne room of his father (Ps. 8:4-5). Jesus is seated at the right hand of God to constantly direct his care towards our lives.

Old wrist watches use to have a spring mechanism that needed to be wind up to be able to keep time. Once the spring mechanism had no more tension to keep the gears going it had to be wind up again to keep the time accurate. God did not "wind up" creation and left it to its own devices until it finally runs out and dies. No. God is constantly at work caring for all of creation.

CREATIO CONTINUA (God continuously creating outcomes for us):

Jesus is constantly at work in creating all kinds of outcomes for us! What is called in classical theology – *creatio continua* – is called in church circles '*testimonies*'. When sometimes a believer addresses the church and shares an unexpected or supernatural personal encounter in regards to Gods intervention, it is nothing less than a witness to God creating an unexpected outcome of some kind. Jesus is extremely creative in creating outcomes that we would normally not for see.

ACTA SALUTIS (God actively saving and redeeming us):

Jesus is seated at the right hand of God where he is actively at work to see people come to salvation, being redeemed from sin and eternal death. Jesus is actively working on Godly appointments and unexpected interruptions in our lives so that we can be redeemed and save not only from the world, but also from ourselves.

CLOSING:

Jesus had to leave to take his place of authority at the right hand of his Father, because there is so much fixing that he needs to do in our broken world. When Jesus walked among men he could at the most touched one person at a time or speak powerfully into the lives of individuals in the crowd. Since Ascension Day, Jesus is on a universal scale caring for all of creation, constantly creating outcomes for the Church and actively saving the lost and redeeming those chosen by the Father. Never ceasing....always at work.

NOTES:

....

....

....

....

....

....

....

....

BEAUTIFUL TRAUMA –
2 Corinthians. 4:1-18/Luke 9:16-17

INTRODUCTION:

Paul's ministry for the Lord was filled among many extraordinary events and outcomes with trauma that he had to deal with. Because of his uncompromising witness and missionary endeavours; due to his calling to serve Jesus Christ he had to face many personal conflicts. He was imprisoned and beaten on many occasions. He was shipwrecked, under house arrest, being left disappointed and neglected by those that he invested in. Trauma was part of his life experience. Partly this was due to the fact that Paul refused to tamper with Gods word when preaching and presenting the gospel, as he was not diplomatic in his approach, but honest and truthful in sharing about Christ. Paul refers in 4:2 to the unethical practice used by wine merchants in his time to dilute wines in creating bigger profit. He on the contrary was always conscious of pure motives in Gods sight.

CONTENT:

The reality is that being human is to be traumatised! When a child leaves the warmth and security of his or her mother's womb on entering this broken world…that child experience his or her first trauma. To be born is to be traumatised! Paul's life and ministry reveals to us that being Christian does not mean being saved from trauma, only from the consequence of sin which is eternal death. In being committed to God we will carry trauma with us! Paul uses an interesting metaphor in referring to him and the apostles as *jars of clay*. This is a common metaphor in the Ancient Near East for describing traumatised individuals (Psalm 31:12-13). *Clay is nothing like stone or steel and leaves an impression of HANDLE WITH CARE!*

In spite of his suffering as an apostle, Paul does not loose heart, because the power of God enables him to endure adversity. *In spite of us being human and having experienced trauma in some way or another we are not defined by any of that...but by the treasure that we carry inside of us!* Verse 6 explains this knowledge: *The ability to sense and understand what God is all about* and not being kept in the dark as those whose "eyes are blinded so that they cannot see the light of the gospel". Jesus is the light to the world and so we carry His light for all to see and to witness.

THE STORY OF "BEAUTIFUL" TRAUMA:

An elderly Chinese woman had two large pots. Each pot hung on the ends of a pole, which she carried across her shoulders. Every day, she used this device to carry water to her home.

One of the pots was perfect and always delivered a full portion of water. The other had a deep crack in it and leaked. At the end of the long walk from the stream to the house, the cracked pot arrived only half full.

For a full two years this situation occurred daily, with the woman bringing home only one and a half pots of water. Of course, the perfect pot was proud of its accomplishments. But the poor cracked pot was ashamed of its own imperfection and miserable that it could only do half of what it had been made to do.

After two years of what it perceived to be bitter failure, the cracked pot spoke to the woman one day by the stream, saying, "I am ashamed of myself because this crack in my side causes water to leak out all the way back to your house."

The old woman smiled and replied, "Did you notice that there are flowers on your side of the path, but not on the other pot's side? I have always known about your flaw, so I planted flower seeds on your side of the path, and every day while we walked back home you watered them and made them grow. For two years, I have been able to pick these beautiful flowers to decorate the table and give to my friends and neighbours. Without you being just the way you are, there would not have been this special beauty to grace our homes and lives."

Sometimes, it's the "cracks," or what we perceive as imperfections, in this reality that create something unexpected and beautiful. These "cracks" allow something to change and ultimately make the whole much richer and more interesting. Everything and every being has its own unique purpose and destiny to fulfil.

Paul does not refer to us carrying water…but light. When we lit a candle in a clay pot without any cracks in it (without it having experienced any trauma like falls or rough handling) is the light visible? NO. But if there are a few cracks in it the light will be projected from within the clay vessel to the outside for everyone to see.

God does not define us by the cracks we have…neither should we. God calls us to be carriers of His light for the world to see (2 Cor.4:6).

Read: Luke 9:16-17.

It was the broken bread that God used to feed the hungry and to perform the miracle of feeding 5000 people. Our brokenness and trauma does not disqualify us from being God's miracle to others.

CLOSING:

WHY I should not let my personal injuries or emotional trauma keep me from being a beautiful vessel to God:

- The more I allow God to use me in spite of my brokenness, the more cause there will be for overflowing thanksgiving to God (2 Cor. 4:15).

- The more I allow God to use me in spite of my brokenness, the more I invest in an eternal glory that far outweighs my challenges (2 Cor. 4:16-17).
- The more I allow God to use me in spite of my brokenness, I allow myself to focus on what is eternal and not only temporary (2 Cor. 4:18). Trauma can last a lifetime, but what God has invested in me will last for eternity.

NOTES:

....

....

....

....

....

....

....

....

....

....

CROWN HIM WITH MANY **CROWNS** – Matthew 2:9-12/21:1-11/Revelation 4:1-11

INTRODUCTION:

Question:

If you had to be one of the three wise men bringing gifts to honour Jesus what would you consider putting down at Jesus feet?

Read: Matthew 2:9-12

The wise men from the East presented the following gifts to honour Jesus:

- *Gold* represents the stature of a *King* (Mat.2:1-2). Jesus the Son of God.
- *Frankincense* was used in the tabernacle and temple in the service of the priests and represents Jesus ministry on earth as Him being the great High priest mediating between man and God (Ex. 30:7-8).
- *Myrrh* is a perfume or fragrance that was used to prepare dead bodies for the grave. This gift represents Jesus mission. Dying on a cross.

These were the gifts that the wise men brought to honour Jesus.

CONTENT:

Read Matthew 21:1-11

When Jesus entered Jerusalem for the last time on his way to die on the cross we read that the disciples and the crowd honoured him by presenting clothes to him:

- The disciples placed their *clocks on the donkey* that Jesus used to ride on as he entered Jerusalem, the capital of Israel. Indicating that Jesus is the true King of Israel.
- The crowd spread their *cloaks on the road* before Jesus. This represented submission to Jesus.
- *Others spread branches on the road.* This is a sign of victory. Jesus is on His way to the cross not so much to die, but to conquer sin and death.

Read Revelation 4:1-11

The heavenly church as portrait by the author of Revelation, reveals to us the elders honouring Jesus by presenting their own crowns to Him:

- 24 elders represents the Church through all the ages.
- Twelve seats represent the 12 tribes of the Old Testament.
- Twelve seats represents the 12 apostles of the New Testament.

You and I were not present at Jesus birth when He entered this world as the King of kings and therefore could not honour Him with gifts. We were not present when Jesus prepared to leave this world when He entered Jerusalem on a donkey, to die. But we will have an opportunity (as we are the church) to bow down in the heavenly court and bring honour to Jesus.

When do I receive a crown? When I die (Rev. 2:10-11/ 2 Tim. 4:6-8). "*On that day*" ... is written in the present passive voice. This simply means that there is already a crown with my name on, but it will only be dispatched when I cross over into eternity to be united not only with Jesus but also with the heavenly Church. That is why in all the letters to the 7 churches in Revelation there is a final word of encouragement to be victorious in the Christian walk. Why? So that we can be presented with a crown.

Now the important question! *WHY WILL I BE PRESENTED WITH A CROWN WHEN ENTERING THE KINDOM OF GOD?* Is it primarily because I lived a victorious Christian life? Or because I lived a life of great faith? Because I am such a gifted minister of the word and gifted with the Holy Spirit or because I am so powerfully used by God to minister to others? NO! I am awarded a crown to safe me from the embarrassment of meeting Jesus face to face and not having anything to honour Jesus with! *IT IS NOT MY CROWN* and it is not presented to me to were for myself....it is to not come in God's presence empty handed! It is to visually acknowledge that it is not about me.....it is all about Him!

CLOSING:

What is the importance of all of this?

- We need to hold steadfast on to the salvation that we have received through Christ atonement on the cross...so that we are worthy to receive a crown of victory.
- We need to get off our high horses. Its time not to be offended so easily because it is not about myself, or my ministry or what God wants to do through me....it is all about Jesus! Whatever praise and honour we are worthy off, we will present that to God. We will take off our crowns and present it to him.

NOTES:

....

....

....

....

THE PENALTY FOR SIN IS **DEATH!** – Psalm 32

INTRODUCTION:

During LENT the Church focus on the effects of personal sin and its devastating consequences on our personal lives, the community and even on our natural resources. Revealing to us why God had to send his Son, Jesus, to pay the ultimate prise for human sin!

CONTENT:

Read: Psalm 32:1

The Old Testament testifies to the reality that true happiness…to really be happy and to experience the peace of God is to know that your personal sin has been taken care of…that your sin has been forgiven and that God does not hold it against you. You are truly rid of the guilt. You are free!

REALISATION: 32:3-4

It was on a Monday morning that the manse in which we were staying at the time, doorbell rang. It was our church youth coordinator who was a personal friend of ours. As he entered the door I knew something was wrong as he seemed to be in distress. As a well-known Christian in town, an active agent in the community, and a successful business man in the Insurance industry, he was finally realising that he was trapped in personal sin to such an extent that there was no way out for him. He did something awful as a Christian that he kept secret from me as his pastor friend, his colleagues at work, his golf partners and his wife and kids for many years. But finally that Monday morning he knew that personal sin had now fully engulfed him. GAME OVER!

CONFESSION: 32:5

As a Christian leader in his own capacity he knew the next step was to confess his wrong doing. To bring all of it into the light (1 John 1:5-10). He confessed to me, then left to go tell his wife and then the people he wronged.

RESTORATION: 32:6-7

Sin always has consequences (Rom. 6:23). It leaves a path of death behind. His marriage was over. His relationship with his 2 daughters took a huge knock. He lost his house…his business and ended up in jail. BUT… God is full of compassion and grace. He delivers and come to our aid in that hour of absolute destitute. As my friend accepted his punishment and willingly worked towards reconciliation with God and others God started doing miracles in his life. Luke 15:17-24 tells us all about restoration.

IMPLEMENTATION: 32:8-10

Today, this friend of mine has been fully restored by God. What he took for granted while serving SIN has been restored back to him. He even has a ministry today where he speaks in church meetings and small conferences instructing people to not go astray as he did and to help others implement into their spiritual life what he learned.

JUBILATION: 32:11

My dear friend is living a life of Jubilation knowing that God has given him a second chance. In Jesus Christ he has been made righteous and upright in the face and presence of God.

CLOSING:

The Biblical process is as follows when we have to deal with personal sin…1 John 2:1-2.

- Realisation
- Confession
- Restoration
- Implementation
- Jubilation

NOTES:

....

....

....

....

....

....

....

....

....

....

EUTHENASIA – A BIBLICAL PERSPECTIVE FROM THE OLD - and NEW TESTAMENT

INTRODUCTION:

Legal assisted suicide is available for almost anyone over 18 - anyone with an "irremediable condition." That could include disabilities; chronic conditions such as asthma, allergies, diabetes or arthritis; degenerative conditions such as poor eyesight; scarring; and mental conditions such as schizophrenia, bipolar disorder, phobias and depression. Any condition can be regarded "irremediable" if a person exercises their right to refuse further treatment. Under this legislation depressed people risk receiving death instead of care and treatment.

Legal assisted suicide is unnecessary, because where assisted suicide is legal, people request death mainly for psychological and existential reasons. Studies show that, when terminally ill people who desire to die receive treatment for depression, 98-99% change their minds. They also change their minds when they receive good care, social support and reconnect with what gives meaning to their life.

We say "yes" to everyone receiving the quality care they need, but we don't believe legalising assisted suicide and euthanasia is in the best interest of society. It would be impossible to enforce safeguards and prevent vulnerable people from being pressured or coerced.

The mere existence of legal assisted suicide would put pressure on some people to request death. Death would be cheaper than ongoing care and in many cases, more convenient for relatives. A person who stays alive would effectively choose to be a burden on society. Legal assisted suicide could also become the ultimate tool for elder abuse.

"A very few 'hard cases' are not a sufficient reason to change the laws that protect everybody. Ending a person's suffering by ending their life is NOT compassion." – The Care Alliance.

CONTENT: A BIBLICAL PERSPECTIVE ON EUTHANASIA:

Read: 2 Samuel 1

The narrator in 1 Samuel 31 says that Saul killed himself. As there is no reason to second guess the narrator's version we come to the conclusion that this Amalekite who was a foreigner (refugee) was lying to gain favour with King David who was most likely to replace Saul as king. The Amalekite lying about him killing Saul was simply an opportunistic scheme thinking that if he could win the favour of David (Saul's rival for the crown) he and his family could gain permanent residency and the fortunate position of protection from David as the future king.

David not being at the scene of the battle, not having the information that the narrator shared with us, he believes the Amalekite's story and version on the death of King Saul. So this morning I invite and challenge you to look at the sanctity of life through the eyes of David.

It is my understanding that in between the time that the Israelites abandoned their towns and fled and the Philistines arrived the next day to strip the dead bodies, this Amalekite (being a refugee) arrived on the scene to search for valuables on the bodies. He then took Saul's *crown* and *armlet* (1 Sam.31:7-8) to present to David.

The words used by the Amalekite in verse 10 carries much resemblance to that used by those supporting Euthanasia in saying: *"Because I knew that after he had fallen he could not survive". Because of the bad prognoses let us put the patient out of their misery…*

What caused David to react in such a strong way when he received the report from the Amalekite?

Verse 14 is very significant in David asking the question: *"Why weren't you afraid to lift your hand to destroy the Lord's anointed?"* Anointed means: *the one set apart for God.* David is confronting the Amalekite in asking: Weren't you afraid to lift your hand against the property of God? In Psalm 139:14-16 –written by David- he expressed that we as humans were created or engineered by God. We carry his design logo. When we lift our hand to assist in helping our fellow creatures to end their lives we cross a clear line.

Verse 10*: "And I took the crown that was on his head..."* We are the crown of God's creation. Psalm 8:4-5 also written by David, makes this statement very clear: *"You have made them a little lower than the angels...and crowned them with glory and honour."* When assisted suicide takes place people are denied bringing glory and honour to God by merely being and existing. We deny our true identity of being the crown of all of God's creation. When we assist someone in suicide we strip them of their crown- the worthy life that was given to them in glorifying God as part of the order of creation.

"And I took the band (bracelet) on His arm..." The arm is the symbol of serving and labour. It is with the strength of our arms and hands that we built, create and serve. The bracelet on Saul's arm was a sign of royalty that he was the chosen one to serve the people of God. When assisted suicide takes place we promote ourselves to being God in deciding when someone is not of use to God anymore! That is not our decision to make.

Read: JOHN 19:17-37

SUFFERING ALLOWS FOR GENIUNE RELATIONSHIPS TO COME TO THE FORFRONT v. 25-27:

In Jesus suffering we see loving human relationships giving meaning to what seemed like a meaningless suffering. Jesus mother, his aunty and Mary-Magdalene support Jesus. Jesus in return makes future provision for his mother (knowing that his death is near). Mary was certainly a widow by now with little or no income and Jesus arranged for her future wellbeing. I believe that euthanasia will compromise relationships and strip people from the emotional and physiological need to depart from one another in a meaningful and secure way.

SUFFERING ALLOWS FOR CARING TO TAKE PLACE v. 28-30:

A jar of wine vinegar was available to Jesus when he said: "I am thirsty." Wine vinegar was used by the Roman soldiers to quench their first. In this situation it was made available to those nailed to the cross. Terminal Illness and suffering allows for much needed and significant care to happen. *Matthew 10:42* states:

[42] And if anyone gives even a cup of cold water to one of these little ones who is my disciple, truly I tell you, that person will certainly not lose their reward."

Jesus promises his disciples that those who care for others, which are especially called by God, will be blessed. Caring for people that are vulnerable brings heavenly rewards to those caregivers. This is no magical trick to get bystanders involved in people's personal injuries and struggles, but a biblical truth that simple witness to the fact that when we show humility to others the blessing in responding to the need (how insignificant even) – will not go unnoticed by God.

GOD DID NOT ALLOW IN JESUS SUFFERING ON THE CROSS FOR EUTHANASIA: v.31-33:

Euthanasia was practised in the Roman Empire on special request and on special occasions. The Jews requested Euthanasia, by the braking of legs, because it was the Sabbath of Passover week. Their request was based on Deut. 21:22-23:

[22] If someone guilty of a capital offense is put to death and their body is exposed on a pole, [23] you must not leave the body hanging on the pole overnight. Be sure to bury it that same day, because anyone who is hung on a pole is under God's curse. You must not desecrate the land the LORD YOUR GOD IS GIVING YOU AS AN INHERITANCE.

According to the above text bodies of hanged criminals were not to defile the land by remaining on a tree overnight. The Romans typically left decaying bodies on crosses long after death to scare civilians from civil offense against the government. However on certain ceremonial occasions such as the emperor's birthday they could take down the bodies, and by breaking the legs could facilitate a quick death by preventing a person from prolonging his life by pushing himself up with his legs to be able to breathe. When the soldiers came to break the offenders legs Jesus has already died. God did not allow for Euthanasia on Jesus.

CLOSING:

In 2 Samuel 1, David wrote a lament to honour the life of Jonathan and especially Saul (2 Sam.1:17-27). In this lament we can sense that David is struggling to come to terms with the death of Saul. Assisted suicide has a tragic result in leaving the family and associates with emotional difficulty and trauma in coming to terms with such an end to life. I believe that it is not only unnatural but also ungodly.

NOTES:

....

....

....

....

....

....

....

....

FACE YOUR **FEAR** AND FIND YOUR **FREEDOM** – 1 Samuel 17

INTRODUCTION:

Israel had a national fear for giants that go back right to the pre-flood period of biblical history.

- Numbers 13: 27-33 is a good example of this.
- *Anakim* means *"long necked" people* which describes tall people or giants that the Hebrews thought were descendants from the Nephilim, who were a powerful race who lived in the pre-flooded world (Gen.6:1-4).
- History repeats itself once again when we read of Goliath in 1 Samuel 17.

CONTENT:

The Nephilim,[16] the product of the sons of god mingling with the daughters of Adam, the great Biblical giants, "the fallen ones," the Rephaim, "the dead ones"—these descriptions are all applied to one group of characters found within the Hebrew Bible. Who are the

[16] Bible History Daily: *The Mysterious Beings of Genesis 6*, Ellen White 05/31/2018.

Nephilim? From where do the "heroes of old, the men of renown" come?

Genesis 6:1–4 tells the readers that the Nephilim, which means *"fallen ones"* when translated into English, were the product of copulation between the divine beings (lit. sons of god) and human women (lit. daughters of Adam). The Nephilim are known as great warriors and Biblical giants (see Ezekiel 32:27 and Numbers 13:33).

It was once claimed that the mating of the sons of god and the daughters of Adam that resulted in the Nephilim caused the flood, and this caused the Nephilim to have a negative reputation. This was believed because the next verse (Genesis 6:5) is the introduction to the flood narrative and because their name means "fallen ones." It is unlikely that this interpretation is correct because Genesis 6:4 presents nothing but praise for the Nephilim and no criticism is present. In addition, the name "fallen ones" is likely a reference to their divine paternity transforming—falling—into the human condition, albeit an almost superhuman condition.

Question:

WHAT FEAR DO YOU ENTERTAIN IN YOUR LIFE THAT KEEPS YOU FROM WALKING FREELY INTO THE PROMISES GOD HAS REVEALED TO YOU? WHAT FEARS DO YOU LIVE WITH THAT IS KEEPING YOU FROM THE PROMISED LAND?

There seems to be one important question to ask when considering this well-known story of David and Goliath. David picks up five stones, but there appears to be only 1 giant! Is David all mouth (1 Sam.17: 45-46), but no muscle? Why does he sound so convincing, but it seems as if he does not really trust God…..why then five stones, but only 1 giant? *Will God dessert us while we are fighting our personal giants? Do we need additional back-up when facing our giants?* One possibility in answering the above question is to consider reading 2 Samuel 21:15-22.

Read: 2 Sam.21:15-22

- There were 4 other, in addition to 1 Samuel 17, horrific giants recorded in scripture that threatened Israel. Did God wanted David to finish them off like he did with Goliath?
- Ishbi-Benob – 21:16
- Saph – 21:18
- Brother of Goliath – 21:19
- "huge man with six fingers and six toes" – 21:20

If this was indeed the case then it matches up evenly....5 stones and 5 giants. Although, David did not in person slaughtered the additional four of these Nephilim according to the account in 2 Samuel 21:15-22, it is clear that Scripture reveals to us that you and I can completely trust on God when fighting and confronting our fears in His honour.

CLOSING:

If we do not allow God to deal with all the fear we carry in our life we will never fully become what God is intending for us to be:

- In our physical state fear protects us from endangering our lives.
- In our spiritual state fear trips us up and keeps us from walking in the fullness of God.

NOTES:

....

....

....

....

....

....

....

FROM THE PLACE OF **GOD** TO THE FACE OF **GOD** – Genesis 28:1-22/32:22-31

INTRODUCTION:

PLACE OF GOD

Jacob was the brother of Esau. Esau was the first born and therefore was the one to receive the blessing of the firstborn according to Hebrew customs. But Jacob schemed Esau out of receiving his blessing by trading Esau's blessing for a bowl of stew (Gen.25:29-33). With the contract of exchange "signed" Jacob was simply waiting for his father Isaac to reach old age so that he could get his blessing to prosper. With Jacob having done his brother in by trading a meal for a prosperous future Esau realised that he allowed his flesh and hunger to come between him and his father's blessing. Things were becoming tense between the two brothers as Isaac was nearing death. Esau realised his mistake and as he was preparing for the blessing ceremony with Isaac, Rebekah their mother came up with a plan to camouflage Jacob as if he was Isaac and the two of them worked out a clever scheme to get ahead of Esau and to take him completely out of the running. Jacob was Rebekah's blue eyed boy and she was willing to lie and cheat with Jacob to see him receive the blessing that was meant for Esau. (Gen. 27: 5-17).

CONTENT:

Genesis 28:1-22

Because of this scheming and cheating Jacob had to flee to start a new life in Northwest Mesopotamia, with Laban, his uncle. His last night in familiar territory, sleeping in the field before crossing the border, he had a God encounter where God appeared to him in a dream and confirmed the blessing of Isaac. The next morning, realising that the *place* where he had slept was a holy place he built an altar for God before setting out (Gen. 28:13-15).

This place (Panim in Hebrew) he called Bethel, (28:16, 17 and 19) is of importance. This was most probably the first time Jacob encountered the living God speaking to him! That is why this place was of such importance to him.

FACE OF GOD – Genesis 32:22-31

Many years have passed and Jacob is blessed with wives, children, slaves and many livestock....he has prospered and is now returning home as God promised him. Just as when Jacob left the land of his fathers, he had a God encounter coming back! Jacob fought with God. He *came face to face with God* and therefore called this place, *Peniel in Hebrew*, meaning to see God face to face.

These two meetings with God-when Jacob was leaving the land and when he returned, reveal to us Jacobs spiritual progression towards the God of the blessing. The progression from hearing the voice of God to coming face to face with Him. The progression from knowledge of God to a revelation from God. *FROM THE PLACE OF GOD TO THE FACE OF GOD!*

CLOSING:

Esau was approaching his brother Jacob with 400 men, and that did not communicate peaceful intentions. However, the anger and hate changed in a moment and the changed happened, because, it was *Israel* (Gen. 32:28) not Jacob whom Esau met. Esau expected to see the arrogant, self-confident scheming cheating brother – instead he saw a humble, repentant man limping toward him and bowing humbly before him (Gen.33:13-14). *No more signs of the impatient, success driven Jacob!*

It took Jacob 20 years, but finally he saw God face to face. Undoubtedly Jacob had been changing throughout all these years. However it is only when he came face to face with the God who spoke to Him twenty years back, that the transformation was complete.... the journey from belonging to believing! From the place of God to the face of God. From knowing the blessing of God to knowing the GOD of the blessing.

NOTES:

....

....

....

....

....

....

....

....

....

....

FISH AND BREAD – A **HEALTHY** DIET FOR A CHURCH-Mark 6:30-44

INTRODUCTION:

Question:

Is fish and bread a healthy died? (In the Mediterranean this could be considered so).

What constitutes or makes a healthy viable church?

CONTENT:

Finding the solution to our challenges among ourselves is a trademark of a healthy and mature church:

Appreciating the resources that God has gracefully provided among us in our mist. The disciples thought that in sending the people away to the food stores will solve the problem. They never thought of searching among the crowd (themselves) for a solution to feed the multitudes. They never considered that the solution to the problem was not out there, but actually "in here!"

"You give them something to eat", Jesus commanded. Jesus was actually hinting that they themselves where the solution to their challenge (6:36-38)! An unhealthy church changes to a healthy church when its members acknowledges that they themselves are the solution to

the problem. The answer is not necessarily and in most cases is not "out there somewhere."

A healthy and mature church always has this great attitude that she will work with what she has:

That was Jesus attitude. He asked the disciples: *"How many loaves do you have?"* When they searched, they said, "*five -and two fish*". Jesus took what was given to him and what was available at that time and turned it into a blessing.

The attitude of thanksgiving or gratitude goes a very long way:

Jesus in the midst of this great challenge directed his focus upwards… giving thanks to God! Expecting a miracle to happen! For healthy churches thanksgiving is part of their spirituality…part of their identity, no matter what season they find themselves in.

Every member contributes to the wellbeing or blessing of the whole congregation:

God does the miracle…we simply distribute the blessing there off. A healthy church is functional, because every member is *contributing towards the blessing or distributing the blessing. A healthy church therefore understands the power of contributing and distributing the gifts and blessing of God! According to the Gospel of John a boy contributed the fish and bread (6:9) and the disciples distributed the food for the miracle to happen! Our church will not see miracles and breakthrough's happen if we do not participate through one of two actions: CONTRIBUTION and DISTRIBUTION! Without these two elements the blessing and the miracle will not happen!*

CLOSING:

Just one illustration: When members contribute funds to their church and the leadership distribute the funds to where the Spirit of God directs…Then the power and blessing of God will manifest! There is only one of two choices you and I have: WE *EITHER CONTRIBUTE TOWARDS THE BLESSING OR WE GO AND BE THE BLESSING.*

NOTES:

INVESTIGATING THE CONCEPT OF JESUS as THE SCAPEGOAT - Leviticus 16:5-10/15-17/20-22

INTRODUCTION:

The word Leviticus translates: *"God calling out to reconcile man with Himself."* The book Leviticus therefore explains the regulations that the community and priest had to comply to in order to be reconciled with God.

Leviticus 16 focuses on the scapegoat's role in making reconciliation possible. Who of you have a scapegoat in your family? That is the person that although may be innocent normally gets to be blamed for everything that may go wrong. Maybe you know such people?

CONTENT:

Read Lev.16:20-21a with Isaiah 53:4-6

According to the prophet Isaiah *Jesus* was lead to be the Scapegoat as already portrait in the Old Testament atonement proceedings.

Read Lev.16:21b with Matthew 26:14-16/47-50.

According to correct procedure, someone with whom a prior arrangement was made by the temple authorities, would take the scapegoat into the wilderness and set in motion the process that will lead to the death of the scapegoat. *Judas Iscariot* was the appointed one that knew prior to Jesus death that he would be the one to set all of that in motion. And so he did. (Hebrews 13:12).

According to research that has been done, the scapegoat is then taken into the wilderness and led up onto a steep cliff. Once on the steep cliff, the person responsible for taking it into the wilderness, pushes it off the cliff to fall to its death. Was Jesus taken up a hill to die? Yes! That hill's name was Golgotha (Place of the skull). Read Matthew 27:33.

CLOSING:

Why two goats?

The one goat is offered as a sin offering and through it being slaughtered its blood washed away the sin and guilt of the people. Representing Jesus covering of our sins by His blood. The other goat was led into the wilderness, onto a high hill and pushed off the highest cliff to fall to its death and in so doing suffered tremendous pain as it laid paralysed awaiting death. In dying, this goat presented Jesus suffering on our behalf and paying the price for our sins.

This ritual was a fore runner to Jesus Christ who suffered on the cross. His atonement on the cross had two specific functions:

- To shed His blood so that our sins could be washed away.
- To die so that we can be made righteous before God.

NOTES:

....

....

....

....

....

A JESUS – CENTRED LIFE
(Are you a triangle or a circle?)
Numbers 2:1-4/10-11/17-19/25-26

INTRODUCTION:

GOD AMONG ISRAEL IN THE DESSERT

The book Numbers tells the story of the second generation of Israelites travelling through the wilderness on their way to the Promised Land. Through a strong visual implementation and demonstration God wanted Israel to understand that He wanted to be at the centre of their life in the wilderness. How did God make this happen? He commanded Moses and Aaron that when Israel was setting up their camp, the family tents were always to be set up in a circle, facing the tabernacle in the middle. With the tabernacle being at the centre of the campsite, it was the embodiment of God being present among his people.

CONTENT:

JESUS AMONG US: John 1:14

"Jesus became flesh and tabernacled (σκηνή = tent) among us" John is describing Jesus, as the son of God dwelling among us, living among us, being with us! Making it concrete he is describing this in the same

way that God in the wilderness centred Himself in the middle of his people. Jesus figuratively has now pitched his 'tent' among us! *GOD IS SO SERIOUS ABOUT BEING IN THE CENTRE OF OUR LIFES THAT HE GAVE HIS ONLY SON TO MOVE IN AMONG US!* In the same way that the Lord was in the centre of the twelve tribes in the desert through the mediation of the tent of tabernacles, so Jesus became God in the Flesh in moving in among us.

JESUS MINISTRY: Mark 1:14-15

This passage brings forth a very tough question? Why would Jesus call on Israel to repent of their sin and turn back to Yahweh? Did God not choose Israel Himself to be a nation from whom salvation would arise? Did God not Himself gave Israel the Ten Commandments, to be able to love and know Him? Did Israel not have priest and scribes to sustain their religion and teachings? In short: *was Yahweh not already their first priority? Was God not the centre of their being?*

Israel understood their relationship with God to be one of a hierarchy with God being their highest priority! Great....what can be wrong then? Israel forgot that God from the time of the wilderness revealed to Israel that He wanted not to be their first priority, *BUT THE CENTRE OF THEIR LIVES.*

Is there a difference? O YES...and a serious difference at that! Israel managed to make God such a high priority in life that it was possible to rank Him out of their ordinary day to day living. With religion it is possible to have God as your highest priority, but yet keep Him out of the centre of your most intimate life!

So then...what was Jesus getting at when he preach that Israel needed to turn back and renew their covenant relationship with Yahweh?

Jesus was reminding Israel that God wanted to be at the centre of their daily lives and not ranked out of it, because of wrong priorities.

CLOSING:

Jesus dies in the middle of two other men....one on His right and one on His left! Finally one last demonstration from God to show the world that no matter how sinful we are HE LONGS TO BE THE CENTRE OF OUR LIFE!

NOTES:

....

....

....

....

....

....

....

....

....

....

JESUS THE **KEY** –
Ezekiel 44:1-3/Luke 19:28-44

INTRODUCTION:

QUESTION

Share with each other a time when you lost your keys and how you managed to find it again….?

Jerusalem was since ancient times the city of God, the central place of worship for the Jewish (also for Muslim and Christian) people. They came to Jerusalem in the times of the feasts, to make sacrifice and to worship. If Jerusalem were too far off, they faced Jerusalem and prayed to God. The temple in Jerusalem was the place and location that all Israelites recognised as the authentic meeting place between God and man.

Jerusalem, still today, has 12 gates whereby the city can be entered. The East gate is as the name suggest on the East side of the city from where she faces towards the Mount of Olives. The East gate was also known as the Golden gate and led directly into Solomon's temple.

CONTENT:

Ezekiel 44:1-3

"Then the man brought me back to the outer gate of the sanctuary, the one facing east, and it was shut. [2] The LORD SAID TO ME, "THIS GATE IS TO REMAIN SHUT. IT MUST NOT BE OPENED; NO ONE MAY ENTER THROUGH IT. IT IS TO REMAIN SHUT BECAUSE THE *LORD, THE GOD OF ISRAEL, HAS ENTERED THROUGH IT. [3] The prince himself is the only one who may sit inside the gateway to eat in the presence of the LORD. HE IS TO ENTER BY WAY OF THE PORTICO OF THE GATEWAY AND GO OUT THE SAME WAY."*

The East gate plays a significant role in the visions of Ezekiel. Ezekiel see the presence of God entering and departing from the temple using the East gate. The approach of the glory of God of Israel takes place at "*the gate facing east."* This is the main temple entrance in the vision, and the equivalent to the gate of the old temple from which God had previously departed (10:19/43:1-5).

Jesus also entered the East gate, when he entered Jerusalem on Palm Sunday just before his sentencing and death, from Bethany which is located on the eastern slopes of the Mount of Olives (*Luke 19:28-44*).

In the year 70 AD the Romans destroyed the city of Jerusalem and ruined the gate. In 1541 when the Turks invaded Jerusalem Sultan Suleiman restored the Golden gate and ordered the gate to be walled up. The Ottoman Sultan Suleiman the Magnificent thus sealed off the Golden Gate in 1541. While this may have been purely for defensive reasons, in Jewish tradition this is the gate through which the Anointed One (Messiah) will enter Jerusalem, and it is suggested that Suleiman the Magnificent sealed off the Golden Gate to prevent the Messiah's entrance.

JESUS WILL ONCE AGAIN RETURN TO ESTABLISH HIS LORDSHIP AND REIGN IN JERUSALEM.

- Zachariah 14:1-5 foretells that with the return of Jesus, he will ascend onto the Mount of Olives. With Jesus putting His feet on the Mount an enormous earthquake will take place that will open the East gate so that Jesus can enter into his royal City that is kept for Him.

- Rev. 22: 16 speaks of Jesus being the Bright morning star.... this star rise in the east.
- Malachi 4:2 speaks of Jesus being the Sun of righteousness... the sun rise in the east.

JESUS WIL ON HIS RETURN NOT BRING THE KEYS TO OPEN THE ENTRANCE TO THE HOLY CITY, FOR JESUS **IS** *THE KEY TO ENTER THE HOLY CITY! WITHOUT JESUS THERE IS NO ENTRANCE INTO THE KINGDOM OF GOD!*

CLOSING:

- *Jesus is the key to enter into everlasting life.*
- *Jesus is the key to enter into a relationship with God.*
- *Jesus is the key to find salvation.*

Revelation 22:14

"Blessed are those who wash their robes, that they may have the right to the tree of life and may go through the gates into the city."

NOTES:

....

....

....

....

....

....

....

....

....

SPIRITUAL **LEADERSHIP** –
Leviticus 8:1-3/22-24/30

INTRODUCTION:

There are 3 ways to find yourself in a position of leadership:

- You made it happen yourself through your personal ambition (Despotic leaders).
- You were placed in such a position not by your own choice, but by the people (Democratic elections).
- You were placed in such a position by God (Spiritual leadership).

In this teaching I shall focus on spiritual leadership and why it is a calling that should not be taken lightly.

CONTENT:

We have read in this section of the ordination of Aaron and His sons. *Why is the sacrificial blood put on the lobe of the ear, thumb and hand?* These 3 areas represent the *WHOLE* person:

- *EAR* is connected to your head/brain which represents your THOUGHTS

- *THUMB* is connected to your hands and arms which represents your ACTIONS
- *TOE* is connected to your feet and legs which represents your WAYS

Aaron and his sons were completely claimed by God and set apart for him and his purposes! God was claiming their thoughts, their actions and their ways! When you are called into Spiritual leadership of some kind you are *FULLY CLAIMED BY GOD!*

The RIGHT *ear, thumb and toe* form a straight line. They are perfectly aligned with one another. The priest had to understand that what they heard God command them to do through their hearing and the way they attended to it through their actions and movements had to be aligned with one another. Meaning that you cannot hear God tell you one thing and you go and do the opposite! Spiritual leadership implies that you are *WHOLE HEARTEDLY CLAIMED BY GOD AND CANNOT FOLLOW YOUR OWN WAYS.*

WHY WAS THE *RIGHT-HAND* SIDE SO IMPORTANT TO BE COVERED IN BLOOD? To understand the importance of this we have to shift to ancient warfare. The right hand side of a soldier was more vulnerable than his left, because soldiers were trained to hold their shield in their left hand and their sword in their right hand. When people fought in Biblical times injuries would in most cases happen on the right side of the body.

CLOSING:

People in *SPIRITUAL* leadership that find themselves in the frontline of spiritual confrontation are more under occult and demonic attack than any other form of leadership and need special covering by God! The Priest where truly key in the religious ceremony of bringing reconciliation between God and man. They needed special covering from God. Those in today's ministries that involves spiritual leadership need it too.

NOTES:

....

....

....

....

....

....

....

....

....

....

A MATCH MADE IN HEAVEN – Genesis 2

INTRODUCTION:

Once a couple was asked what is the secret to their marriage as they were married for almost 70 years. Expecting a decent answer the husband came up with a surprising quick and short reply: "That is easy he said…the answer is simply: 'YES DEAR.'" Those of us that are married know that this is not as easy as assumed in the husband's humorous reply. Marriage is not only a big commitment it is also an enormous responsibility.

CONTENT:

According to Genesis chapter 2 we find God creating and establishing the following:

God created *beauty* ("pleasant to the eye" = beauty – Gen 2:9).

God created *prosperity* (Gen 2:12).

God created *meaning* (Gen 2:15, 19). Giving Adam a sense of purpose and a sense of calling.

God created *community* (Gen 2: 20-23).

God created *intimacy* (Gen 2:24-25).

In chapter 3 of the book of Genesis we find that Satan appears on the scene with one very specific goal and that is to attack and eventually destroy what God had created. Why is Satan so focussed on destroying marriages? For Satan to destroy the best of God's creation he only needs to focus on destroying one aspect of God's handy work in order to destroy all of it! What do you think that is? Marriage!

When Satan manages to break up marriages he manages to undermine all of God's hard work in creation. Let me explain:

Is there beauty in marriage? YES! When you are truly in love and committed to someone all of life seems beautiful. This may be a time when couples are mostly absorbed in the presence of their love one, but for them it is the most exciting and beautiful time of all. Seeing an old married couple walking down the street and holding hands after many years of marriage is to say the least is beautiful!

Can marriage bring prosperity? YES! If you know that your husband or wife loves you even in spite of your weaknesses, you have the freedom to be all that God wants you to be....you can be prosperous. You have the freedom to excel.

Can marriage be meaningful? YES! Caring for and loving someone else are acts of meaning in themselves. Adam cared for God's creation and that in itself gave Adam a sense of purpose.

Can marriage give one a sense of community? YES! For marriage drives away loneliness and creates a sense of belonging.

Can marriage be the answer for our human need for intimacy? YES! To have that understanding that my husband or wife know me better that any other person...knowing my most inner being. The word *intercourse* in Hebrew is translated as to mean: *knowing your significant other in the most intimate way possible.*

Marriage signifies all of God's creation in one. For Satan to destroy marriages is to destroy all of God's creation!

CLOSING:

Three ways to safeguard our marriages as being the most beautiful creation of God:

- Never stop investing in your marriage…as God never stops to care for his creation.
- Never stop praying for your marriage…Jesus never stops interceding for us.
- Never stop supporting one another in marriage…as the Holy Spirit never stops to be our helper and comforter.

NOTES:

………………………………………………………………………………………………

………………………………………………………………………………………………

………………………………………………………………………………………………

………………………………………………………………………………………………

………………………………………………………………………………………………

………………………………………………………………………………………………

………………………………………………………………………………………………

………………………………………………………………………………………………

………………………………………………………………………………………………

………………………………………………………………………………………………

NO RISK… NO REWARD –
Ecclesiastes 11:1-10

INTRODUCTION:

A retired wheat farmer once told me many years back he had one of his best crops on the field that specific year. The Sunday after church he pulled out his Mercedes and told his wife to hop in as he wanted to take her for a drive through the crops to show her the majestic lands. That afternoon he promised her the latest Mercedes model from the dealer's floor once the crop was cleared and the money in his account. That same night bad weather developed and hail stones as big as tennis balls destroyed all of his investment that year on the land. "Farming is like gambling for you just never know how it will work out for you in the end," he concluded his story.

CONTENT:

Ecclesiastes 11:2

Life produces its share of calamities and disasters. Things do not always go according as planned. That is why we have life insurance and why it is such a profitable business! *LIFE simply HAPPENS!*

Ecclesiastes 11:3

*Many aspects of life cannot be changed as it is a given...*we can simply not do anything to change it. Gravity is a given fact. When clouds get to heavy gravity pulls them down in the form of rain. When an enormous tree falls down the gravitational force on it is so huge that the only way to move it is for the forestry foreman to cut it up in logs and to shift it off.

Ecclesiastes 11:4

There is never a perfect time...if we keep on waiting we shall lose out on living. We all have experience of procrastinating. Longing for change, reward and positive consequences; but not wanting to put in the hard yards and commit ourselves to whatever it takes. There is no use in expecting results without working towards it.

Ecclesiastes 11:5

We will never managed to answer all of life's questions or that of the universe. Some things we know with certainty and some things we don't. In the field of medical science it still is a wonder and a miracle of life for a baby to grow inside a mother's womb and eventually be born. The Godly engineering that takes place in the womb still amazes medical scientist.

Ecclesiastes 11:6

Results are never guaranteed. My parents always told me: "Do not count your chickens before they hatch." There is no use in starting off well, but not attending in diligence to the end. Without also finishing well, is there no guarantee that the results will be what you are expecting or hoping for.

Ecclesiastes. 11:7-10

Nothing ever stays the same...change is unavoidable. Aging is a proper example. It is only when we reach our 40's that the reality slowly, but surely sets in that we cannot take our health for granted. Our metabolism slows down. Depending on what we eat, we gain wait and physical activities that we use to do without giving it much consideration can now become an effort.

So what now? Do we stop living and start hiding?

Ecclesiastes. 11:1

> *"Ship your grain across the sea;*
> *after many days you may receive a return."*

LIVE CONFIDENTLY! TAKE A CALCULATED AND BRAVE STEP FORWARD. LIFE IS A GAMBLE BUT YOU CAN ONLY GAIN FROM IT IF YOU STEP OUT INTO IT AND EMBRACE IT!

The Levities stepped into the Jordan River while it was in flood and in so doing managed to be the first tribe of Israel to lead all of Israel into the Promised Land. Their risk to trust God paid off.

Peter was the only disciple who stepped out on the water with Jesus. And although this experience would only last a few seconds, walking with Jesus on water empowered him to become the first New Testament Apostle to step out on Pentecost day in the chaos the Holy Spirit brought about, seeing 3000 Jews on one single day come to faith.

Although, Jesus was to be killed...he stepped out in the direction of the cross on the hill knowing that although everything seems so senseless and wasted that He was about to save the world.

CLOSING:

A small family business was soon to be wiped out by the coming of property investors wanting to build a mall exactly were the family has been doing business for many a year! Many other surrounding businesses took the money offered them by the gigantic investing company and left their business, but this owner had no such plans. Due to sentimental reasons he wanted to keep his business going for his children's sake. The property investors had no choice but to shift their project just next door from this owner...leaving the small family business in the shadow of the huge mall being erected next door to it. Instead of feeling devastated the owner tried to think of a plan of managing to not only survive for the future, but to make a strong recognizable input. He had a plan and decided to put his plan into action at the right time. On the day that the mall had its grand opening he erected a huge sign at the entrance of his shop reading: MAIN ENTRANCE TO MALL AREA!

No risk…no reward!

NOTES:

....

....

....

....

....

....

....

....

....

....

WHEN **ORDINARY** BECOMES EXTRAORDINARY – Matthew 7:21-29

INTRODUCTION:

Question:

Why is the supernatural ministry of the church an important part of our witness?

It is a showcase to the unbeliever that the kingdom of God is powerful and that it has truly come near! For believers it is encouraging as we realise that although we are still human and living human lives on earth, we have already transcended into the presence of God. It is very exciting to pray for healing and it happens, or when we speak truth into someone's life and it produces Godly results!

CONTENT:

However, the test for true discipleship lies not exclusively within the reality of the supernatural, but where ordinary Christian living becomes extraordinary commitment to God!

In the Sermon on the Mount Jesus spells out what true discipleship looks like:

- To let your light shine before others (stepping into human darkness and bringing hope)-4:16.
- To live according to the 10 commandments-5:17-20.
- To let go of anger-5:21-22.
- Protecting marriages in our church from adultery and divorce-5:27-32.
- Keeping to our promises (I shall pray for you….) – 5:33-37.
- To not want to justify ourselves-5:38-42.
- Love our enemies-5:43.
- To give to the needy-6:1-4.
- To pray and fast-6:5-24.
- To not live a materialistic lifestyle-not to try and keep up with my neighbour, but to lead thankful lives in regards to what we have-6:19-24.

Does this sound to ordinary for the Christian life? O no! Most of us fail at these challenges!

When we master ordinary Christian obedience, we start living extraordinary lives for God!

HOW CAN I START LIVING AN EXTRAORDINARY LIFE FOR GOD?

- By acknowledging that God uses my ordinary Christian obedience and turns it into extraordinary results.
- By acknowledging that when we master the ordinary Christian lifestyle we bring honour and blessing to God.
- By acknowledging that it is not the supernatural that impresses God, but ordinary Christian obedience that becomes extraordinary commitment to God.

CLOSING:

John 6:1-15 is an example from the Gospels where *Jesus feeds the 5 thousand.*

- A boy contributes, in obedience, his lunchbox with 5 loaves and 2 fish to Jesus.

- Jesus takes the boy's offering and through prayer commits it into the Fathers hands.
- Then the kingdom of God sets the supernatural in motion and this boy's ordinary obedience leads to an extraordinary festival with loads of food.

NOTES:

....

....

....

....

....

....

....

....

....

....

GODS **PERFECT** TIMING – Luke.3:1-6

INTRODUCTION:

When we have a personal word from God either through scripture or through prayer we can become filled with a sense of expectancy! Waiting on God to bring His word for us into fulfilment. Unfortunately as the time passes and days become weeks, weeks become months and months become years we lose that sense of expectancy and either think that we are at fault or God has it all mixed up!

To understand all of this we need to acknowledge the difference between the Greek words *Chronos* and *Kairos.*

Chronos is linear time and well presented in the form of wearing a wrist watch and following a calendar. This is time represented in exact seconds, minutes, hours and days and so on……

Kairos is to be understood as the opportune time, supreme moment or fitting time. Kairos represents a time requiring decisive action as it represents a window of opportunity.

CONTENT:

God's dealing with us as his children and his church is in general not primarily *Chronos*-time as it is *Kairos* time that takes us into new spiritual seasons and fulfilment. The Bible does not give us a precise day or time when Jesus will return. In the words of Jesus the Bible commands us to always be ready for the Lords return (Matthew 24:36-37/25:13). Muslims have to pray 5 times a day at precise moments, but Paul instructs us to pray at all occasions, constantly.... with no reference to time. Prayer is supposed to be a part of our spiritual, in the moment, responsibility.

God is well into *Kairos* time, meaning God is always first setting the stage, getting all in place for the most fitting event to happen. When the Godly appointed time arrives God is ready to act in our lives. How old was Caleb, for instance, when God set the stage for him to collect his promised section of land? 80 years (Joshua 14:10-12)! Was God concerned for Caleb at that age? No! It was at that given time that the Kairos time emerged. The stage was set for Israel to finally establish themselves in the Promised Land and take it from its former inhabitants.

Luke 3:1-6

Tiberius Caesar:

From the Mediterranean world and well into Africa and Europe nations were in the hands of the Roman Empire. The Caesars were the 'gods' of the known world and idol practices were widely introduced in all the cities and regions of its influence. The people of Israel were under this foreign rule and its identity and religion under pressure from Rome. The so-called, *Pax Romana*, which means the *peace of Rome* was a false peace whereby every nation that was willing to identify with Rome and bow the knee before Caesar would be protected by Rome and its authorities. The world was governed under a false sense of security and the stage was set to introduce the real Prince of Peace, Jesus Christ on to the scene! *The stage was set. Kairos time!*

Pontius Pilate:

He was the governor of Judea and the future judge in the trial of Jesus. He was all for pleasing the Jewish authorities on preventing any uproars in his governance that could prevent him from climbing the Roman corporate ladder. The stage was therefore set in Judea for Jesus to arrive, to be judged and crucified by the governor so that salvation could come to all of humanity. Pilate was destined to be the representative of Roman authority in sending Jesus to his death. *Kairos time* indeed.

Annas and Caiaphas

Both Annas and Caiaphas were the high priests of this particular time. Relieving each other in this position. They had to play the key role of convincing the Jewish community that Jesus was a fraud and a danger to their system of belief. According to the prophet Isaiah, chapter 53 the Son of God had to experience the wrath of God and the rejection of His own people. Who would be in the line-up for that? Annas and Caiaphas! *The stage was set in the local context, whereby Jesus own people were ready to see him die.*

CLOSING:

The stage was indeed set, with all the necessary characters, to introduce Jesus to the world....in more precise language: The opportune time arrived to announce the long awaited coming of our Lord Jesus.

When you are carrying a word from God or a promise from the Holy Spirit you will soon become discouraged if you count the days on the calendar or the years that has since gone by. Rather focus on how God is setting the stage to release His word onto you at that Kairos moment-at that specific Godly appointed time!

NOTES:

....

....

....

....

....

THE QUEST: TO BE OR NOT TO BE? – MARK 3:7-19

INTRODUCTION:

In one of Shakespeare's plays called Hamlet the issue of life (To be) and death (Not to be) is compared and tossed around to come to grips with the reality of death and the true meaning of this life. Today we shall try to come to grips with what does it mean to be Christian and to identify with the Church?

CONTENT:

In the calling of the twelve (Mark 3:13-18) Jesus appointed the disciples for 3 specific tasks:

- To be with Him
- To preach
- To do spiritual warfare

Mark makes it very clear to us from the very beginning of his Gospel presentation that Jesus is *relational* (Mark 1:14-15) and that TO BE with JESUS is very important to God. The Gospel of Mark states very clearly that primarily Jesus calls us into his presence and transform our lives, first and foremost to be *with Him* and only then secondary to be in ministry and service to Him.

We are first called to be with Jesus and only then to be the church!

WHAT DOES IT MEAN TO BE WITH JESUS? According to *John 17:3* it means to *know* Jesus. The Greek word that is used in John 17:3 (Yίνῳσκῳ) does not refer primarily to intellectual knowledge, *but knowing a person through direct personal experience*, implying a continuity of relationship. This is the kind of knowledge you can only incur through spending time with someone. In *Matthew 7:21-23* the same word is used when Jesus says: *"I never knew you."*

There is no merit in it for us when we know how to be the church without knowing what it is like to be with Jesus! Our primary calling as Christians is to be with Jesus so that we know Jesus as our Saviour, as the Son of the living God (Matthew 16:13-17)!

"John 14:3 ...and take you to be with me...." To be with Jesus (through studying his word, prayer and meditating)...is preparation for heaven! Jesus is preparing a home for us in Heaven to simply be with Him!

CLOSING:

In verse 20, following on our reading for this message, mention is made of the *crowds.* Jesus ministry graciously included those that would follow him from an impersonal crowd.

The *crowds* (*Ochlos* in Greek), when mentioned in the Gospels do not represent those formally identifying with Jesus, but rather following him from a distance. Not knowing him, but only associating with him out of curiosity. *Ochlos*, refer too many that were only interested in the works of Jesus like healing and setting people free...not taking the time to know him as their Master or Messiah.

In the Gospels the writers use the word: *Mathetes (Disciples)* to indicate those followers with a genuine intention of getting to know Jesus in gradually coming to faith in him as the promised Messiah.

We have two options: becoming a disciple and make a decision to get to know Jesus. OR remain part of the crowds and only experience him operate from a distance.

NOTES:

....

....

....

....

....

....

....

....

....

....

GOD'S **RETIREMENT** PLAN FOR HIS PEOPLE – Revelation. 21:9-27

INTRODUCTION:

Question:

Who has a retirement plan in place? Who is not planning for retirement and believe that they will simply "expire" when the time comes?!

Today we shall be looking at seven institutions that you will not find in the New Jerusalem.

CONTENT:

Pastors/preachers and prayer warriors will be out of a job or ministry: 21:18-21

No more vacant positions in that department. See *Ex 28:17-20 with Rev. 21:19-21*. The stones that was embroiled on the breastplate wore by the priests in the Old Testament will be used to decorate the city walls in the New Jerusalem. Why is this important? The Old Testament priest was representing the people in the presence of God. Only the high priest could enter the holiest area of the temple and once he entered he was representing the whole of Israel in the presence of the almighty living God.

All believers will now be constantly in the presence of God and will not be needing people to intercede for them or to be taught on how to have a relationship with God. You will not find individuals there called to ministry because everyone will be worshipping God *(Zechariah 14:20).*

There will be no more churches to attend: 21:22

We will be in an undisturbed relationship with the Father, the Son and the Holy Spirit and will have no need for the intervention of the church and its ministries. See *John 4:21 (Zechariah 14:9).*

There will be no prisons because there will be no more sin: 21:23

For sin to exist it needs darkness. Jesus will be the Lamp constantly supplying holy light in the city and in so doing will be shining forth the holy glory of God the Father. As there can be no darkness in the presence of God and sin needs darkness to maintain its power, sin will not be able to affect us any longer (*Zechariah 14:6-7*).

There will be no more war: 21:24

All nations will live in the glorious light of God. No more time will be spend by nations on weaponry and to train skilled soldiers, but to enhance the glory of God and His Kingdom *(Zechariah 14:16).*

Evil will be no more: 21:25

Because sin will not be able to exist without darkness, Evil will not be able to affect us. Therefore, the gates of the city will never be shut, because no evil will be able to enter it, as it will no longer exist (*Zechariah 14:10-11).*

There will be no more scarcity of food to only be able to get by 21:26

The nations will bring their wealth and resources into the New Jerusalem and lay it down before the throne of God. *See Matthew 2:2/11.* In verse 26 the word *tee-may' (*τιὴν*)* is used which can be translated into the English language as: *Valuables*

There will be no more police: 21:27

Criminality will be no more! (*Zechariah 14:21c*).

CLOSING:

Revelation 21 is reminding us that no matter what kind of retirement plan we have organised for this life that heaven's plan for us, on spending eternity with God in his "resort", outweighs all other human initiative. We do need to plan for retirement and we do need to have our ducks in a row, but the ultimate retirement scheme that beats all others is the one that God is preparing for us *(John 14:1-3).*

NOTES:

....

....

....

....

....

....

....

....

....

....

"I **SURRENDER** AL…" - Philippians 2:1-11

INTRODUCTION:

When we study the Gospels and especially the references to Jesus suffering and humiliation we tend to come to an understanding of the perfect way that Jesus surrendered to the will of his Father. Being obedient in not only following his Father's instructions on departing from such a glory, but on entering such a broken and unfair world as the one we life in.

CONTENT:

Selfless love: vv6-7.

Verse 6-7 refers to the waiver of the rights and privileges of Jesus Christ to live in the glory of the Father... to simply let go of His heavenly privileges. Jesus willingly gave up, renounced the glory thereof, and was presented in human likeness into the womb of Mary through the intervention of the Holy Spirit to be born in Bethlehem! God in and through Jesus Christ left home to pitch his tent among mortal man. In classical theology we refer to *this as the emptying of Christ ...the humiliation of Christ whereby he revealed to us his selfless love without primarily considering his true identity or origin.* Heaven's loss became our gain when the angel Gabriel announced to Mary:

"*You will conceive and give birth to a son, and you are to call him-Jesus.*" The birth of Jesus Christ is nothing less than God reaching out to us!

Servant heart: v.8

Verse 8 reminds us that we cannot acknowledge the *crib*, but reject the *cross*! We simply cannot celebrate Christmas and ignore Passover! Grace comes at a cost! To be made righteous before God, the wrong must be corrected and Jesus served that purpose by dying on a cross. When Mary placed Jesus in the crib, Jesus journey to the cross was activated. *The incarnation of Jesus lead to his humiliation!* Heaven became bankrupt when Jesus was conceived so that Jesus could declare on the cross: "*Tetelestai*"...It is finished...*the outstanding account of sin has been paid in full!* Jesus did such a complete and final work on the cross, because he loved us unto death. In dying he portrait his servant heart: "*Greater love has no one than this: to lay down one's life for one's friends (John 15:13).*

Surrender: vv.9-11

Just as the crib activated the cross, so the end purpose of the cross was the exaltation of Jesus! *The purpose of Jesus humiliation was his exaltation.* Paul now in the last verses is making a statement in saying: *if this is the character of God; if he revealed his selfless love to you...if he emptied himself for you by dying with a servant heart on a cross...then he deserves your surrender! Give it up...it is worth it! Is this not the kind of King you want to serve? One with no self-interest. One who willingly gave up his heavenly bliss and sinless environment to come to your and my rescue? One who willingly offered himself so that we could have a future...an everlasting one!*

CLOSING:

The story of Jesus is one of the *Crib ... the Cross ... and the Crown.* Because Jesus took on the crib, the self-emptying and denying of himself he proofed himself to be worthy of the cross. In his obedience to his heavenly Father, he who is God, gave it all up for the sake of rescuing all of creation. He died obediently. Therefore, Jesus is exalted at the right hand of his Father as he will rule over all nations, tribes and people.

NOTES:

....

....

....

....

....

....

....

....

....

....

TAKING ON THE UNEXPECTED BRICK WALLS IN OUR LIFE – Exodus 13:17-14:31

INTRODUCTION:

At last Israel was free from Egyptian slavery and free from bondage as they set out for the Promised Land. Well....almost free and maybe not yet fully on their way as they would have expected...suddenly they had to face and cross the Red sea! Talk about unexpected brick walls!

To turn back was not the ideal option as that would entail moving back into a life of slavery, misery and no future expectations. Moving to the left or to the right would entail moving deeper into the dessert and that could mean dying of starvation or lack of water. Facing the vast expand of water seemed the only option moving forward. What can we learn from scripture and to be precise from this challenge that Israel had to face when we hit those unexpected brick walls?

CONTENT:

[17] When Pharaoh let the people go, God did not lead them on the road through the Philistine country, though that was shorter. For God said, "If they face war, they might change their minds and return to Egypt." [18]

So God led the people around by the desert road toward the Red Sea. The Israelites went up out of Egypt ready for battle.

Trust God for the way forward...he knows best. Stay calm, carry on and don't look back!

21 By day the Lord went ahead of them in a pillar of cloud to guide them
on their way and by night in a pillar of fire to give them light, so that
they could travel by day or night. 22 Neither the pillar of cloud by day nor
the pillar of fire by night left its place in front of the people.

God will direct the way. For Israel to see God's directions they had to look UPWARDS and FORWARDS to see the cloud pillar and the pillar of fire. Do not become a slave to circumstances that wants to bring you down. Don't look back! More importantly... don't look down!

*14 Then the Lord said to Moses, 2 "**Tell the Israelites to turn back***
and encamp near Pi Hahiroth, between Migdol and the sea. They
are to encamp by the sea, directly opposite Baal *Zephon. 3 Pharaoh*
will think, 'The Israelites are wandering around the land in confusion,
hemmed in by the desert.' 4 And I will harden Pharaoh's heart, and he
will pursue them. But I will gain glory for myself through Pharaoh and all his army, and the Egyptians will know that I am the LORD." So the Israelites did this.

When God gives instructions like: OK...*turn back* and it simply does not make sense or seem right at the time, put your faith in action, because *GOD HAS GOT THIS!* He is working his plan!

13 Moses answered the people, "Do not be afraid. Stand firm and you will
see the deliverance the Lord will bring you today. The Egyptians you see
today you will never see again. 14 The LORD will fight for you; you need
only to be still."

***GET OUT OF GOD'S WAY.* Do not override God's plan by making your own or thinking you know better. WAIT and see God at work!**

15 Then the LORD said to Moses, "Why are you crying out to me? Tell the Israelites to move on.

YOUR CALLING AND PURPOSE IS BIGGER THAN YOUR CRISIS*...get on with what God has called you too. God will deal with your impossible brick wall and you get on with life. In the Hebrew language it implies something like: *pull out the tent supports, pack up and move on...

[19] Then the angel of God, who had been traveling in front of Israel's army, withdrew and went behind them. The pillar of cloud also moved from in front and stood behind them, [20] coming between the armies of Egypt and Israel. Throughout the night the cloud brought darkness to the one side and light to the other side; so neither went near the other all night long.

You and I can reckon and count on God's supernatural protection: He is the best at strategic warfare!

[29] But the Israelites went through the sea on dry ground, with a wall of water on their right and on their left. [30] That day the LORD saved Israel from the hands of the Egyptians, and Israel saw the Egyptians lying dead on the shore. [31] And when the Israelites saw the mighty hand of the LORD displayed against the Egyptians, the people feared the LORD and put their trust in him and in Moses his servant.

The purpose of brick walls in our lives is to build our faith and trust in God.

CLOSING:

Stay calm and trust God for an outcome.

Look upwards and not towards the over powering circumstances.

Put your faith in action when it seems useless.

Get out of Gods way as he works his plan.

Get on with serving God – your calling is bigger than your crisis.

God will protect you – He knows what you are up against.

Keep your focus: Brick walls only purpose is to build our faith in Gods abilities.

NOTES:

....

....

....

....

....

....

....

....

....

....

JONAH "DOWN **UNDER**": Jonah 1-4

INTRODUCTION:

In the Hebrew language the word: *YARAD* means to "*go down*" or "go under".

The word *ALAH* has the opposite meaning of "*going up*" or "*being exalted*".

These two expressions or words are crucial and key in reading the story.

Jonah had to go *up* to Nineveh, the great capital of Assyria, but he travels *down* under to Joppa. He "*YARADS*".

Jonah's situation gets worse as he "*YARADS*" into a further downward spiral when he moves from the deck of the ship downwards below the deck area to sleep in not having to face the consequences of his disobedience as the stormy weather builds outside.

Jonah "*YARADS*" even further down into misery when he is thrown overboard...down into the dangerous sea!

This is what happens when you have a word from the Lord to attend to, but you rather ignore it. Your life moves into a downward spiral motion which keeps on dragging you down into misery! So why was Jonah so reluctant to go preach on the topic of repentance in Assyria?

Assyria was a powerful enemy to Israel and Jonah new that God was slow to anger and merciful. Should the Assyrians repent on behave of his preaching, then God surely would show mercy and not go through with destroying Assyria. This would have been bad news for Jonah, because he would prefer seeing Assyria destroyed and removed from the landscape altogether. With this in mind Jonah not only flee from his task, but also from God.

CONTENT:

God directed Jonah to Nineveh to preach repentance, but Jonah did not obey and therefore God had to go to extreme measures. In casting lots, Jonah was found to be responsible for the storm at sea and was thrown overboard. Jonah was saved in an unusual way by a whale and God gave Jonah three days to repent before Jonah was released from the belly of the whale back on shore.

God made a deal with Jonah. He did not have to go back to Nineveh to preach a *sermon* but only had to go back to deliver a *message* containing only 8 words: "*Forty more days and Nineveh will be overthrown*".

The results were extraordinary!

- A whole city repented!
- The King of Assyria in person called on God.
- Even the animals in Nineveh broke down before God!

What can we learn from these extraordinary outcomes in Nineveh?

- If you and I have a calling from God, we better do something about it as God will not back down. He will give us gracious time to repent and to make up our minds, but will be back calling us.
- If God can accomplish such extraordinary results from un-motivational obedience consider what God can accomplish through committed obedience to Him!
- God's grace and mercy is all enduring and able to reach those that least expect or deserve it.

CLOSING:

Theologians make a comparison between *Jonah* and *Jesus.* Especially, in regards to the three days Jonah spend in the belly of the huge fish and Jesus spending three days in the grave. The comparison is clear, but the difference even more so:

Jesus *ALAH* (was lifted up) onto a cross in obedience to the call of his Father, because God was concerned for the state of the lost.

Jesus spend three days in the grave to be *ALAH* (lifted up from the dead).

Jesus ALAH into heaven after forty days where he is seated at the right hand of God.

NOTES:

....

....

....

....

....

....

....

....

....

....

VERBALLY ARTICULATING THE GOSPEL: BY INVITATION. Luke 14:15-24

INTRODUCTION:

Just this week the Breakfast news team on TV wanted to take a survey in regards to the upcoming Easter holidays. Should chocolate making companies take out the word: "*Easter*" from the packages the chocolate is distributed in so that it says chocolate bunnies and not *EASTER CHOCOLATE BUNNIES*? The news team were claiming that the Easter Christian story is outdated and that people do not believe the claims to salvation that Christian Churches proclaim during the Easter weekend. I don't know what the outcome of the viewer's response was, but what I do know is that as the public sector becomes more and more secularised that society and our communities in society, will become totally disconnected from the story or Christian narrative of Christ, because even the sentiment and symbols in society that reminds us of our Christian heritage is being removed. What will this eventually come to? *THE LOCAL CHURCH BEING THE ONLY PLACE WHERE THE GOSPEL COULD POTENTIALLY BE CLEARLY ARTICULATED AND EXPLAINED.*

Verbally articulating the gospel is central to reaching the community. This can happen in any situation, whether a formal gathering like a church service, or in a conversation at home, at work, or in a social setting. As we are called to give witness to Christ, so we must take the responsibility to be equipped – knowing the gospel and understanding how to go about it.

Connecting with our community is about hospitality. Essential to evangelism is *invitation.* Jesus' Great Banquet parable speaks of a God who invites the community to a great feast. A servant is directed to invite all kinds of people to the feast. We are called to serve in this way, and invite people to join God in his great restoration project. Certainly, evangelism includes inviting people into a personal relationship with God. However, it does include basic hospitality. It is inviting people to be a part of a people, God's family, and the local church. All humanity is invited as the gospel is a radical vision of people of every race, age, men and women, rich and poor, together as one.

CONTENT:

The first striking fact that comes from this parable is that the way to enter into the Kingdom of God (The life of Christ) is primarily by invitation (Lk. 14:15).

The way the Church goes about its business in the community is always by INVITATION and never by OBLIGATION (demand).

Expect excuses and lies as we invite and welcome others into our community of faith (14:18-20):

- You don't buy property and a section of land and then afterwards only go to look at what you have purchased.
- You don't buy oxen and then only want to find out how healthy and fit they are after the purchase. You always test drive a car before you buy it.
- In the Old Near East biblical towns were small which meant that according to custom almost all the people will attend a wedding or big social event that is on the calendar. It is impossible to have more than one social event on at any

given time. This man in the parable would unlikely organise a banquet knowing the wedding feast will last about 2 weeks.

The host is persisting in finding guests: We should choose wisely in considering those we invite (14:21).

- The poor cannot use the escape route of lying and saying they need to go and see the land they bought.
- The crippled cannot use the excuse of buying oxen and have to go and try them, because a crippled cannot walk behind the oxen and steer them to plough the land.
- The lame person cannot use the excuse of celebrating his or her wedding as lame people would not be able to marry as they were socially ranked out of society.

Never give up be as persistent as the host in this parable.

CLOSING:

What influences people to come to Church?

Advertisement = 2%

Organised visitation = 6%

Pastoral contact = 6%

Invitation from a friend = 86%

The majority of unchurched people do not come to church seeking to grow spiritually or to get saved from hell. They come to connect with others…as in the popular theme song of the old "Cheers" TV show, people are looking for "A PLACE WHERE EVERYBODY KNOWS THEIR NAME AND EVERYBODY IS GLAD THEY CAME."

NOTES:

....

....

....

....

....

....

....

....

....

....

TWO KINDS OF DEVOTIONAL **WORSHIP**

INTRODUCTION:

Where will you place your worship of the Lord?

Intimate and personal?

OR

Charismatic and outgoing?

CONTENT:

THE MARY-TYPE WORSHIPPERS:

Read John 12:1-11/Luke 10:38-42

Nard is an oil producing plant which produces an extravagant aromatic oil. The content of the jar was very expensive. Mary did something that was a sign of honour in ancient society. *In Judaism hair was associated with a woman's glory, herself-worth and self-respect.* Not only did Mary pour an extremely expensive ointment on the feet of Jesus, she also used her hair to wipe the oil that did not get absorbed into Jesus' skin. *In other words she placed her self-worth at his feet, she gave him her riches and her glory. IT WAS AN ACT OF SILENT DEVOTION TO GOD.*

When we read Luke 10:38-42 we get some better insight into the personality of Mary. She was into personal devotion to God. To sit all by herself at Jesus feet and shut the world out was her preferred style of devotion and worship to God. Jesus endorsed that kind of worship: Lk.10:41-42 and Jn.12:7-8.

THE MESSIAH-TYPE WORSHIPPERS:

Read John 12: 12-19

Many Jews were travelling to Jerusalem for the Passover festival. Jesus was also on His way to Jerusalem not to celebrate Passover but to fulfil Passover by dying on the cross. Some of these Jews recognised in Jesus person and ministry those symbols and signs that is accredited to the coming messiah and did recognise Jesus as such. They started shouting: HOSANNA, meaning: SAVE US! Then they took palm branches and went out to meet Jesus, acknowledging Jesus to be a king that will rescue the Jewish nation from Roman authorities… saving them from being enslaved to such a heathen ruling nation. It was like an uproar because the crowd was loud and proclaimed the glory of Jesus to those who wanted to hear and those who did not! It was like an open air, public worship service…proclaiming publicly the glory of Jesus. *THIS WAS AN ACT OF PUBLICLY DECLARING GOD'S PRESENCE AND POWER.*

CLOSING:

In the Bible there is clearly room for both spirituality's.

Therefore there is room for both spirituality's in church.

Let's identify the Mary-type worshippers and the Messiah-type worshippers.

Let's acknowledge the differences.

Let's celebrate those differences.

NOTES:

X-AMOUNT OF SIN - John 19:28-30

INTRODUCTION:

Question:

How do you pay your monthly accounts? Cheque, cash or the internet? In the following teaching we will rediscover how Jesus went about to pay for our outstanding account of sin. It is therefore almost impossible to appreciate John 19:28-30 without investing some time on the issue of personal or private sin.

28 Later, knowing that everything had now been finished, and so that
Scripture would be fulfilled, Jesus said, "I am thirsty." 29 A jar of wine
vinegar was there, so they soaked a sponge in it, put the sponge on a stalk
of the hyssop plant, and lifted it to Jesus' lips. 30 When he had received
the drink, Jesus said, "It is finished." With that, he bowed his head and
gave up his spirit.

Does personal or secretive sin have the ability to mount up to a large outstanding number as when you do a count? Yes…I believe so.

James 5:20

"Remember this: Whoever turns a sinner from the error of their way will save them from death and cover over a multitude of sins."

Plethos in Greek reads: *"large number or multitude of sin"*. Let us look at it from a different angle: Does the Bible explain sin in economic terms....like numbers or amounts? Yes...I believe so.

Romans 6:23

23 For the wages of sin is death, but the gift of God is eternal life in Christ Jesus our Lord.

Opsonion in Greek reads: *"pay or wages."* This Greek word also has the meaning of conveying a certain cause or result. Thus explaining that the result of working on behave of sin is a pay check or wages that brings forth death! It is clear that the Bible do speak of sin in the context of economic terms like numbers and wages.

CONTENT:

In reading John 19:28-30 we find the word: *finished/fulfilled* are used 3x! Now will you believe me if I tell you that in the Greek New Testament the word *finish* is an economic term: *Tetelestai.* It means: *The outstanding account (debt) has been paid in full! This word: Tetelestai, derives from the world of economics and finance. We are forgiven...we do not need to live a life of constant guilt before God. We have been shone mercy and forgiveness. Whatever I was in debt before God was taken care of by His son Jesus Christ on my behalf! Jesus came to clear your and my name from being black listed!*

Colossians 2:14

14 Having cancelled the charge of our legal indebtedness, which stood against us and condemned us; he has taken it away, nailing it to the cross.

Due to our outstanding sin account we were heavily in debt with God. If we owe someone money we can be prosecuted according to the law. That was our position before God, but Jesus took it and paid that outstanding sin account in full with his own precious blood!

***ACTIVITY**: Give everyone a piece of paper and let them write a number down what they perceive as a possible reflection of their sin –debt account* *with God. Then let them cross [X] the amount out and write over it – "my debt has been paid in full." Tell them: "What you have just done or experienced is what the Bible teaches us is CRACE!*

CLOSING:

- *Grace comes at a high cost – it does not come cheap*. Jesus paid with His own death and cleared your and my X-amount outstanding sin-debt with His own blood. When it is your birthday and you receive a gift you are not expected to pay for it, but simply to graciously accept it…the cost thereof has already been paid for.
- *Grace is free.* That is why we call it 'grace' – meaning it is *undeserving goodness!*
- *Grace is dangerous***.** Read Matthew 18:23-35. If you and I know that Jesus has settled our outstanding account with God he is expecting from us to do the same in regards to our fellow men.

NOTES:

....

....

....

....

....

....

....

....

....

....

WE SAY "YES" TO THE LIGHT – Revelation 1:9-20/21:23-25/22:4-5

INTRODUCTION:

The book of Revelation is not only one that needs to be interpreted from within an understanding of symbols and its symbolic meaning for those at the time that it was written, but also that the symbols are keys to understanding what is implied.

The following are some symbols that are important in interpreting the topic at hand.

Jesus:

- "*Dressed in a robe reaching down to his feet*" implies Jesus to be the High Priest.
- "*Golden sash around his chest*" implies that Jesus carries Godly authority.

The Church:

- "*Golden*" lampstand. Gold is valuable (Every congregation is valuable to God).
- Gold is a valuable commodity (Every congregation is valuable to God, because it was bought/accumulated at a high price).

The Angels:

- They are in Gods Right hand which implies that they are under God's authority.
- They are in Gods Right hand which implies that they are under God's protection.

CONTENT:

WHAT DOES EACH OF THESE SYMBOLS HAVE IN COMMON?

Jesus, the church and the angels are portrait as being at work, projecting and spreading light!

Jesus:

- *Is described in terms of light: eyes = blazing fire (v.14), feet = glowing bronze (v15) and face = brilliance of the sun (v.16).*

When Jesus was taken up into heaven it was not only to be seated at the right hand of God to intercede for the church, but also to make his presence felt *in* the church. When He ascended into heaven he did not forget his people, but has taken his place among his church to shed light on our ministries and to guide is in times of darkness (v.12-13).

Church:

- *Lampstands are being used to radiate light where it is dark.*

Jesus spoke to John in this vision and as John turned around to see who it was that he heard speaking, he saw Jesus among the lampstands (v.13). What is significant about this is the fact that John did not see Jesus at first sight, but could recognise him only by the light that was generated by the lampstands! It is through the light that the church generates from within its ministries of outreach and evangelism that the world will come to find Jesus! See Matthew 5:14-16.

Angels:

- *Stars shine the most brilliantly when it is the darkest of nights.*

God directs his angels to strengthen the church in its roughest and toughest hours. When human support is not sufficient anymore... God supplies supernatural intervention....his angels to bring light into our darkest situation. See Hebrew 1:14

CLOSING:

In the book of Revelation we find that chapter 1 relates to the theme of light. Then follows utter darkness as the anti-Christ appears on the scene with the 7 seals being opened and devastation setting in on planet earth. Only in chapter 21/22 – the final chapters -do we find the theme of light coming into its rightful place again. For example: 21:11/21:22- 24. As well as 22:5/22:16

Revelation 21:10-11 New International Version (NIV)

10 And he carried me away in the Spirit to a mountain great and high, and showed me the Holy City, Jerusalem, coming down out of heaven from God. 11 It shone with the glory of God, and its brilliance was like that of a very precious jewel, like a jasper, clear as crystal.

Revelation 21:22-24 New International Version (NIV)

22 I did not see a temple in the city, because the Lord God Almighty and the Lamb are its temple. 23 The city does not need the sun or the moon to shine on it, for the glory of God gives it light, and the Lamb is its lamp.
24 The nations will walk by its light, and the kings of the earth will bring their splendour into it.

Revelation 22:5 New International Version (NIV)

5 There will be no more night. They will not need the light of a lamp or the light of the sun, for the Lord God will give them light. And they will reign for ever and ever.

Revelation 22:16 New International Version (NIV)

16 "I, Jesus, have sent my angel to give you this testimony for the churches. I am the Root and the Offspring of David, and the bright Morning Star."

NOTES:

....

....

....

....

....

....

....

....

....

....

ZERO AGE RESTRICTION – Numbers 13:26-30/14:23-24 and Joshua.14:6-15

INTRODUCTION:

The story of Caleb stepping into God's promise and purpose for his life is called: *possession by faith!* Caleb primarily relied on God's promise when asking for territory. Not his age or the risk he soon had to face could scare him off. His focus was on his Godly inheritance.

The narrative in Numbers 13:26-33 tells the story of twelve spies. Ten of them were focussing in their report on BIG giants and a little God. Two spies (Caleb and Joshua) were reporting on their return on their BIG God and little giants! They believed that God could be trusted.

CONTENT:

HOW DID CALEB MANAGE TO FOCUS ON GOD'S **promise** IN HIS ADVANCED AGE?

- *He kept his faith active according to God's word and promise no matter how long it took (Jos.14:10-12).*
- *He shared his expectation not only with God but with others (the tribe of Judah) - being accountable to them in regards to what he expected. (Jos.14:6).*

- *He kept physically healthy and fit* (Jos.14:11).
- *He acknowledged the authority and blessing from his leader-Joshua* (Jos.14:12).
- *He kept a fighting spirit* (Jos.14:11-12).

The Anakites descended from Anakim (meaning "long necked" or tall). The Hebrew people thought them to be descendants from the Nephilim, a powerful giant-like race in the pre-flooded world. This was the supernatural race Caleb had to face and fight in order to receive his long awaited inheritance. For forty five years Caleb had built on this promise which God gave him. He believed the promise, and waited patiently for its fulfilment and when the hour came, he put in his claim and God honoured it.

CLOSING:

God is never late, although it may seem to us at times that God has forgotten his promise or word to us!

Even in our old age can we expect God to surprise us and at the same time be on time for us.

NOTES:

....

....

....

....

....

....

....

....

BONUS EDITION:

SERMON SERIES

SPIRITUAL GIFTS – SUNDAY 1

Introduction to spiritual gifts and understanding their importance

INTRODUCTION:

Question:

How do you prefer to fly abroad? Business class, first- or economy class?

The first time my mother travelled alone by plane she thought that you fill the plane starting from the front to the last back row. Not realising that on a plane you have business class in front, after that first class and then economy class, she took a seat in the business class section. Problem was that her ticket was allocated for the economy class! She was friendly escorted by the flight attendants out of business class to the back of the plane where the rest of the economy seats was to be filled.

Unfortunately, this is how we sometimes perceive and conceptualise the distribution of spiritual gifts to believers, by the Holy Spirit. Even if we don't say it we think it and in worse case scenarios some churches even proclaim it. What am I referring to? That some of us are labelled as having the best spiritual experiences and gifting's and therefore are somehow business or first class travellers and that others have to do with what the Holy Spirit has left in its gift room and simply are second or third class Christians because it seems that we either have insignificant or no spiritual gift!

CONTENT:

In Joel 2:28-29 it is promised that God will direct the Holy Spirit to bring restoration to all people (all flesh). *All GENDER (men and women), AGE (young and old) and CLASS (even servants) is included in this promise.*

The Holy Spirit and Its gifts is intended for every believing individual!

What about the four key nationalities or "people groups" that is well represented in the New-Testament?

- *Jews (Acts 2:1-5)*
- *Samaritans (Acts 8:1-8, 14-17)*
- *Romans (Acts 10:1-3, 44-46)*
- *Greeks (Acts 19:1-6)*

They all witnessed the outpouring of the Spirit. *The Holy Spirit and Its gifts is intended for every believing nationality!*

Closing:

In understanding that the Holy Spirit is not keeping Himself or His spiritual empowerment from us lets investigate into the meaning and purpose of the spiritual gifts.

NOTES:

....

....

....

....

....

....

....

SPIRITUAL GIFTS - SUNDAY 2

INTRODUCTION:

1 Corinthians 12:1-11

In my first congregational ministry I had the opportunity to preach during the Pentecostal week of prayer. In sensing that the Holy Spirit wanted me to help members come to a real practical understanding of His presence and support I laid hands on a lady in the service and she was instantly healed. She rang me the following day to thank me and to praise God. From this experience I have learned two lessons:

- We don't own spiritual gifts…it owns us.
- The purpose of having and using spiritual gifts is to bring honour and praise to God.

1 Corinthians 12:4-6 is crucial and key in understanding the different areas of gifting:

- 1 Cor. 12:4 - *gifts* (*charismatic or supernatural*) that we read of in 1 Cor. 12:1-11.
- 1 Cor. 12:5 – *service* (*diakonia or practical service*) that we read of in Rom. 12:1-21.
- 1 Cor. 12:6- *activities* (*energema or tasks*) that one is called to) that we read of in Eph. 4:11.

Let's consider the Charismata or charismatic gifts.

CONTENT:

Knowledge:

With God having absolute perfect knowledge on all things, and with us having knowledge levels that are completely imperfect and limited, this means that we all need to receive words of knowledge from the Lord on a very regular and frequent basis in order to be able to safely journey through this life.

The Word of Knowledge is simply the Holy Spirit transmitting His specific knowledge to you on something that you would have no ability or means to be able to know about with your own limited intelligence and current experience.

It is supernatural knowledge and insight being given directly to you by the Holy Spirit Himself, not by your own mind or your own intelligence.

This supernatural information is what I call the "inner knowledge". All of a sudden, you will receive a: *without-a-doubt* type of sensing in your spirit perceiving that the Holy Spirit is trying to transmit information to you. It can come in the form of a thought or an impression on your mind, or possibly come in the form of a vision or a picture in your mind's eye.

Wisdom:

This next gift at times will work in conjunction with the *word of knowledge*. Sometimes, all you need is a direct word of knowledge from the Holy Spirit and it will completely solve the problem or dilemma you are dealing with. However, there will be other times that a word of knowledge will not be quite enough to solve the problem. This is where you will now need a word of wisdom. A word of wisdom will give you the ability to properly apply the knowledge that you may already have in a particular difficult situation. For instance, if someone gives you a car instruction manual that will show you how to restore a car engine, that manual will give you all of the actual information you will need to understand in how to do it. But all of that knowledge will not do you any good unless you have a sense of where you need to start and how to proceed to eventually be able to appreciate and enjoy the final product as described and explained in the manual. If you can understand what you are reading, then the next and crucial step will be to have the actual wisdom to be able to actually restore a car engine out in your garage once you try and do it. All of that knowledge from the car manual, and all of that understanding of that knowledge will do you no good in real life if you do not have the wisdom to be able to apply that knowledge to a real life working situation.

Faith:

This supernatural faith does not refer to salvation, but faith to accomplish some task that demands one to step out in faith and rely on Gods promises. This refers to those situations that ask for an action or response without having sufficient information or proof.

Gifts of healing:

Notice that the wording being used in this verse is that this is the *"gifts"* of healing. The word *"gifts"* is plural, which means there are different kinds of healings the Lord will want to do. People, with this kind of anointing, have found that some will be more gifted and anointed in some areas than they will be in other areas. Because God is creative in many ways, His creativity also applies to the subject matter of healing those that are in need. For instance, some people may have more success with healing bad back cases, where another may have a stronger anointing to heal cancer cases. In other words, the Lord will sometimes specialize on the kinds of healings He will want to do through an individual believer.

Miraculous power:

Our God is a miracle-working God and He still loves to do them for His people. The Bible says that God does not change, and if both Him and Jesus were constantly doing miracles in both the Old - and New Testament, then God will also be wanting to do miracles in our day and age.

Prophecy:

Prophecies from the Lord can cover an extremely wide range of situations and issues. Covering everything from predicting future events like they use to do in the Old-Testament, to giving someone counsel, encouragement, confirmation, instruction, and possible correction when it may be needed.

Distinguish between the spirits:

This next gift is one that is really needed in the dangerous and perilous times that we are now living in. The first thing to notice about this gift is that the "s" in the word "spirits" is with a small "s." This means that it is not referring to the Holy Spirit. The only other spirits that this gift is referring to are the following three kinds of active spirits:

Demons
Angels
Humans

The Holy Spirit provides supernatural discernment, insight, and knowledge involving these three kinds of spirits. Many of the times, this gift will be used to fully expose what spirit is at work and what kind of spirit is operating and therefore responsible for causes, behind the scenes.

Tongues:

It will be a "foreign" language that you will not be able to speak by your own ability. Only the Holy Spirit's supernatural transmission of this language out of your spirit will give you the ability to be able to speak this language in a specific context and in specific situations. And whatever tongue the Holy Spirit will give you, you will be able to use it 24/7, as necessary. It will be your own personal, private, prayer language between you and the Lord.

The only challenge with this gift is that for the most part, you will never know or understand what you are interceding on God's behalf for. Either a specific occurring event, spiritual attack or significant happening that needs special covering and intersession at a specific time.

The Bible informs us that we will be speaking out "mysteries," and only God the Father and the Holy Spirit will know the reason and necessity for having us pray in that manner. If we do not know exactly what we are praying about when using this gift, then why would God even want us to have this kind of a gift in the first place? I believe the reason is in the verse- Romans 8:26- where it says that sometimes we will not know how to pray as we ought to. Sometimes, we will not be able to find the right words to use in our own personal prayers to the Lord due to our own natural imperfections in being able to properly communicate with Him.

Interpretation of tongues:

This gift application is where the Holy Spirit will give you the interpretation of the tongues that you have either prayed on your own or when they are being done by someone else in a worship service setting. There are two main criteria in the Bible instructing us on how to minister and conduct the actual manifestation and occurring of this gift:

"If anyone speaks in a tongue, let there be two or at the most three, each in turn, and let one interpret. But if there is no interpreter, let him keep silent in church, and let him speak to himself and to God" (1 Corinthians 14: 27-28).

"Therefore let him who speaks in a tongue pray that he may interpret. For if I pray in a tongue, my spirit prays, but my understanding is unfruitful" (1 Corinthians 14:13-14).

CLOSING:

Paul placed the last 2 gifts at the end of the list because an overemphasis on tongues in Corinth had led to the neglect of those other much needed gifts.

NOTES:

SPIRITUAL GIFTS – SUNDAY 3

INTRODUCTION:

Romans 12:1-2

To the Greeks the spirit mattered most and not so much the body (flesh). In fact for the Greeks the body was a prison to be ashamed of. We saw last week in 1 Corinthians 12 where Paul had to address the Greek Christians on the topic of spiritual gifts and that the one gift was not more important than any other, because the spiritual gifts are all given to the glory of God and to the encouragement of all. Now in Romans 12 Paul is stating that our bodies – our physical existence is just as important to God ("*offer your bodies as a living sacrifice*"), because it is through the functions of our bodies that we can serve in the most practical ways. To put it differently, Paul is urging the believers in Rome to actively contribute to the life of the church according to the measure of faith that God has given each of them, by serving one another as a sacrifice to God. When we commit our live to God we do not only give Him the control and access of our spirit but also our physical strength and capabilities.

CONTENT:

Do you need a physical body to serve others and to be able to enriche their lives? YES! How can you dish up a meal if you do not make good use of your hands? How can you pass on a cup of tea or water to someone in need if you do not commit your hands to be of service? Do you need sacrificial hands to start the lawn mower that will get the lawns done at church before Sunday? Do you need sacrificial hands and a willing body to set out rows and rows of chairs for a funeral? Yes! Do you need a willing body and sacrificial hands to arrange flowers for the next Sunday meeting? Yes! Let us not forget about cleaning the toilets and keeping an eye on the bins that need to be emptied from time to time! *Our bodies enable us to get on with the demands of life. Offering our bodies to God enable us to live sacrificial lives! Our theology becomes distorted when we prioritise the spiritual over and above the call to serve others in the most simple and practical ways. This touches on the importance of faith and deeds as explained by James in his letter in chapter 2:14-26.*

If the Holy Spirit has called you into leadership how can you couch and mentor someone without being physically present in that person's life? Biblical leadership is not dictatorship and giving orders from the top down…it is discipleship by sharing life with those that you need to direct and lead.

How do you show mercy to someone…by helping them? By doing something for them. Your physical presence and intervention is what is asked for.

CLOSING:

Science has revealed that a premature baby, born a few weeks or months too early and therefore having to stay in an incubator for some time, will speed up there growth and development double as fast when experiencing physical contact. The parents can pray and even the local church can pray. The parents can invest money and transfer their baby to an even better hospital or fly in a world renowned medical practitioner to secure that their baby will live. Primarily it is when the parents sacrifice their time to spend each day in hospital and to physically be present in a serving and nurturing capacity that the health of the infant start to improve.

It is when Children of God offer our bodies as a sacrifice to God and to one another that the church grow in unexpected ways! (12:4).

NOTES:

....

....

....

....

....

....

....

....

....

....

SPIRITUAL GIFTS – SUNDAY 4

INTRODUCTION:

Ministry gifts- Ephesians 4: 1-16.

In the Biblical time of the Old Near East nations would constantly be at war with one another. The victor, at war, will take the targeted city captive by enslaving the people living there and take for his kingdom gifts from the captives palace or temple sites (Ps. 68:18). Paul uses Psalm 68:18 and rephrases it in saying in Ephesians 4:1-16, that Jesus as the Victor on the cross ascended to heaven and is seated at the right hand of God the Father from where he gave gifts to his Church. What is Paul implying? *CHRIST BLESSED THE CHURCH WITH MINISTRY WORKERS/ THE GIFTS TO THE CHURCH ARE THOSE CALLED TO MINISTRY:*

- Apostles
- Prophets
- Evangelists
- Pastors
- Teachers

CONTENT:

Apostles (Messengers), help the church to grow *broader.* They bless the Church in *expanding its influence* in initiating new ministries and developing Kingdom minded strategies for the body of Christ – locally and globally.

Prophets, help the church grow *stronger (closer)* to God as they call Gods people (back) to the purpose of pursuing God and not the world. Prophets are the conscience of Gods people as they warn us when we tend to lose sight of our commitment and love towards God.

Evangelists, help the church grow *larger*. They are mostly responsible for exponential growth in our churches and are not only motivated to see the pews filled on any given Sunday, but also motivated in seeing people enter the kingdom of God through repentance and renewal to God.

Pastors ("shepherds") help the church grow *warmer*, because of them establishing a caring and protective environment. Pastors' main calling and ministry is to protect members in their spiritual development and lead the congregation according to the instructions of the Word and Spirit.

Techers help the church grow *deeper into the knowledge of God.* The Bible is not a straight forward "manual", but rather a complicated read at times. It takes time, dedication and discipline to read, understand and teach the Bible in context and in regards to its full content. Without the knowledge that fuels ongoing discipleship we cannot move into the more advanced things of God.

- *Apostles* – support the Church in growing *broader* (expand its influence).
- *Prophets*- support the church in growing *stronger* (closer) towards God.
- *Evangelists*- support the church in growing *larger* (exponentially).
- *Pastors* – support the church in growing *warmer* as we are encouraged to care.
- *Teachers*- support the church in growing *deeper* into the knowledge of God.

CLOSING:

The word: "one" is used 7 times. 7X is the number for God. The unity among us in spite of different gifts/services/workings reflects the harmony we have in God and our love for one another.

NOTES:

....

....

....

....

....

....

....

....

....

....

SURVIVING YOUR SPIRITUAL DESERT – SUNDAY 1

INTRODUCTION:

Exodus 25:1-40

What does it mean to find yourself in a Spiritual desert or to experience spiritual oppression? In very general terms it means that it is too hard to continue on your way to reach your destiny or to complete your task at hand. It means that you have considered giving up on the mission or journey that you are on. In more specific terms it could mean considering to give up on God, on the Church, your marriage, your children, your parents and in severe cases giving up on life.

Over the next few Sundays, I am going to help you find some stepping stones in your spiritual desert to not only find some grip and firm ground from where to continue, but some inspiration to continue on your path.

Before we start it is important to acknowledge the following:

- We are not supposed to stay in the desert…it is only temporarily…as it is a means to an end (Exodus 13:17-18).

- The desert is our place of preparation (Exodus 3:1-10). If you are in a spiritual desert at this time the question you and I need to ask God is: *FOR WHAT PURPOSE?*

CONTENT:

As Israel started their journey in the desert God commanded them to make an Ark, a Table and a Lampstand (*In the following presentation I shall change the order of symbols for the purpose of my conclusion).*

The Ark:

Verse 19-20 give instructions on making two cherubs of gold to be placed on the atonement cover of the ark. These Cherubs were angelic figures with the task of protecting the content that was kept in the Ark. There is a resemblance with Gen.3:24 when God placed Cherubs at the entrance to the Garden of Eden to protect the tree of Life.

In the ark the two stone tablets with the 10 commandments was to be kept safe. The 10 commandments is a resemblance to the *TREE OF KNOWLEDGE OF GOOD AND EVIL* (Gen. 2:9).

The Lampstand:

The Lampstand had seven lamps and God took seven days to complete creation-Gen.2:2

The Lampstand is shaped in the figure of a tree and represents the *TREE OF LIFE*-Gen.2:9

Question:

The construction of the *Ark* and the *Lampstand* has a strong connection with the Garden of Eden. Is that intentional? Israel, as portrait in the book of Exodus, is in a desert and their circumstances that they have to deal with has absolutely nothing to do with paradise! Or does it?

It is to remind Israel that although they find themselves NOW in an isolated desert, that God was about to reinstate the blessing of the Garden of Eden to them on entering the Land of Milk and Honey. The desert is their place of preparation not their place of destination!

The Table:

The Bread of the Presence was so-called because it was constantly exhibited before the Lord. It consisted of 12 loaves to have been laid in piles of 6 each. The bread was a symbol and reminder to Israel that although they found themselves in the desert that God will sustain them and provide for them.

For those of us that are in a spiritual desert this is a symbol of the sustenance and refreshment that God offers us in spite of being emotionally and spiritually challenged.

CLOSING:

What do I need to do to survive during my time in this spiritual desert?

- Allow God time and space to meet with you as he did above the Ark of the Covenant with the High Priest (Exodus 25:22), to talk to you and to encourage you.
- The bread on the table is a reminder of communion and it points to Jesus as the bread of Life. Don't neglect church gatherings and to join in with communion as this is to support us in gaining spiritual sustenance.
- The Lampstand and the oil to make it burn represents the Light and guidance of the Holy Spirit. Be aware that the Holy Spirit will lead and guide you at all times.

NOTES:

....

....

....

....

....

....

SURVIVING YOUR SPIRITUAL DESERT – SUNDAY 2

INTRODUCTION:

Exodus 28:6-43

In Exodus 28 like in the previous chapters on setting up the Tabernacle (Tent of meeting) the colours ***gold, blue, purple and scarlet*** are the key colours to include into the making of the Garments for the Priest. *Gold represents God's beauty, Blue represents God's divinity, Purple His royalty and the colour Scarlet His power.* These materials imply that the priests are close to God and act as his representatives to the people.

CONTENT:

The jewels on Aaron's robes represent the 12 tribes of Israel, on whose behalf Aaron enters Gods presence. The breast piece is to have 12 different stones set in four rows of three, each with the name of one of the 12 tribes. This piece among others indicate that he is to act as a representative on behalf of the 12 tribes to bring them to remembrance into the presence of God

Exodus 28:9-11

[9] "Take two onyx stones and engrave on them the names of the sons of Israel [10] in the order of their birth—six names on one stone and the remaining six on the other. [11] Engrave the names of the sons of Israel on the two stones the way a gem cutter engraves a seal. Then mount the stones in gold filigree settings [12] and fasten them on the shoulder pieces of the ephod as memorial stones for the sons of Israel. Aaron is to bear the names on his shoulders as a memorial before the LORD.

The above instruction has immense spiritual meaning. The High-priest who was set apart to represent the people (12 tribes) before the Lord was instructed to "*carry*" Israel on his shoulders. It meant whenever the High-priest started his shift, put on his garment and entered the presence of God, he was "*carrying*" Israel on his shoulders to remind God that He has promised to never forsake His people but to "*carry*" them through the desert. God was reminded that if He did not "*carry*" Israel on His shoulders like the priest did figuratively they would not survive the journey *["Shoulders" is where we "carry" our cross or burdens].*

Exodus 28:29

[29] "Whenever Aaron enters the Holy Place, he will bear the names of the sons of Israel over his heart on the breast piece of decision as a continuing memorial before the LORD.

This also carries immense spiritual weight. When the High-priest entered in His official capacity the presence of God he was "*carrying*" Israel figuratively on his heart! In so doing the High priest was reminding God that Israel was His first and true love. That if God stopped caring and stopped loving Israel they simply would not be able to continue on their own. *["Heart" is where we "carry" our emotions].*

Question:

Who according to the New Testament is our High Priest?

Hebrews 4:14

[14] Therefore, since we have a great high priest who has ascended into heaven, Jesus the Son of God, let us hold firmly to the faith we profess.

Question:

When you were wandering in your spiritual desert who reminded God to not stop supporting and loving you? Jesus our High Priest.

Hebrews 4:15-16

[15] *For we do not have a high priest who is unable to empathize with our weaknesses, but we have one who has been tempted in every way, just as we are—yet he did not sin.* [16] *Let us then approach God's throne of grace with confidence, so that we may receive mercy and find grace to help us in our time of need.*

Hebrews 6:19-20

[19] *We have this hope as an anchor for the soul, firm and secure. It enters the inner sanctuary behind the curtain,* [20] *where our forerunner, Jesus, has entered on our behalf. He has become a high priest forever, in the order of Melchizedek.*

CLOSING:

If you are now in a spiritual desert. You need to know that you are being loved and cared for by God, because your High Priest has entered the presence of God to remind Him to be mindful of you.

NOTES:

....

....

....

....

....

....

....

SURVIVING YOUR SPIRITUAL DESERT – SUNDAY 3

INTRODUCTION:

1 Kings 19:1-18

Elijah had great "mountain-top" experiences with God during his profound course of ministry. He experienced the miraculous provision of God and even the raising of a dead child. The most powerful experience was the one being on the mount of Carmel when he called on God to proof Himself over and against the Baal prophets and afterwards saw to it that the Baal prophets were killed at the end. But no matter how many great mountain top experiences we have it still is only down in the desert that we *GROW*! (Chapter 18).

Soon after the dramatic Carmel episode we see a different character in Elijah as he plan to flee from Jezebel. Jezebel had a consistent track record of disposing of the Lords prophets and he ran to flee from Jezebel, knowing that he was next inline. He flees from Jezreel in the North to Beersheba in the far South of the Promised Land. Approximately 193 km.

CONTENT:

In the beginning of chapter 19 we read that Elijah found himself burned out and depressed. Elijah thought that he will end it all by deserting into the dessert (19:4). *Not realising that the desertedness of the wilderness would be the place that God had chosen to minister to him (19:6-8). It is when we come to the end of ourselves that God finally is given the chance to intervene. (Matthew 5:4).*

Our spiritual desert is very often the place where God releases his angels to support us: (Hebrew 1:14). When you and I have been deserted by man and we have no one to count on heaven releases an angel when we the least expect it. The angel protected Elijah while he was a sleep as well provided provisions in the desert to keep him alive.

Our spiritual desert is often the place to receive new revelation:

Horeb is another description for Mount Sinai where God revealed Himself to Israel through the Mosaic Covenant in giving the 10 commandments. Elijah is on his way to Horeb, because God is about to reveal Himself again. It is striking that after Elijah had already travelled almost 200 km the angel mobilises him to travel another 400 km to reach the mount. Sometimes we want to come out of our spiritual desert as quickly as possible, but forget that as it is a place of revelation that we should not want to leave until we have received direction from God.

To hear the voice of God, to receive the blessing of new direction and revelation especially while journeying through a spiritual desert we need to seek *silence.* You may not hear God's voice for new direction at the next big Evangelical/Pentecostal convention with its loud gospel bands that seems to be able to shatter rocks and shake up your struggling walk with the Lord. I am very doubtful that the charismatic speaker being on fire himself will be able to change your situation…when you are in the desert, you need to hear from God Himself and therefore you and I need to embrace Silence at such a time.

CLOSING:

The desert does not define us. God's intention is neither to leave us to perish in our spiritual deserts, nor to be stuck without clear indications for the future or a new way moving forward. God's provision and support in times of spiritual struggle is real and surprising for us.

NOTES:

....

....

....

....

....

....

....

....

....

....

SURVIVING YOUR SPIRITUAL DESERT – SUNDAY 4

INTRODUCTION:

Luke 4:1-13

Our spiritual deserts can be intimidating to say the least! To feel deserted, isolated, having lost the sense of purpose and direction and having to deal with conflict and pressure at the same time can be overwhelming. Some time it is in the making and we can anticipate a desert journey coming on…other times it is the element of surprise that propels us into our desert uninvited.

Luke mentions that, for Jesus on entering into his first physical as well as spiritual desert, that there was no surprise there as we have just read in Luke 4:1 that it was(most probably) the Father that decided to put the desert journey on Jesus itinerary and it was the Holy Spirit that led Jesus into the desert! *This desert was Godly intended. But WHY?*

Just previously Jesus had his baptism where the Holy Spirit descended on Him and empowered him (*Luke 3:21-22*) and immediately after reading of the desert experience we read that Jesus started with His teaching ministry (*Luke 4:14-15*). So why did Jesus had to have an intimidating desert experience after receiving the companionship of the Spirit, but before being released into the public? Is it not enough to have the Spirit of God to step into ministry? Is it not enough to have the indwelling of the Holy Spirit to get on with the challenges of life? Apparently not! The Father wanted Jesus to be subjected to character development. *Simply put: God interrupts our lives by allowing spiritual deserts for the sole purpose of developing and growing our godly characters. We have mentioned this before...GOD IS NOT PRIMARILY INTERESTED IN THE POWER ENCOUNTERS THAT WE HAVE IN OUR DAILY WALK WITH HIM, BUT IN THE PERSON WE BECOME!* God never tempts us to do evil, but he does use intimidating desert experiences to develop us into the people he has called us to become.

Romans 5:3-5

3 Not only that, but we rejoice in our sufferings, knowing that suffering produces endurance, 4 and endurance produces character, and character produces hope, 5 and hope does not put us to shame, because God's love has been poured into our hearts through the Holy Spirit who has been given to us.

CONTENT:

Moses was a man with a prestigious CV. He was well educated in the school where Egyptian royalty where trained and educated. He was not only trained in academic knowledge considered important for his time, but also trained in international affairs and protocol. As Moses had the *right qualifications* it seemed that he was God's man for the task of leading God's people to freedom.

Moses must have *loved* his fellow countrymen. He not only tried to bring reconciliation between two Israelites fighting, but even murdered an Egyptian mistreating one of the Israelites. Moses felt such a strong connection with his own that he put himself at risk protecting most probably a slave worker. He not only had an impressive CV, but his social action for social reform on behalf of those not as fortuned as he was, was honourable!

One could even go so far as to call Moses sentiment towards his people as having a *calling* to serve them, where it is recorded in Acts 7:25 "*Moses thought that his own people would realize that God was using him to rescue them...*"

Moses seemed to be the man...Gods man for the task of setting Israel free from generational bondage into slavery. Wrong. Moses lacked the most important of all principles: *AUTHORITY. "But the man who was mistreating the other pushed Moses aside and said, 'Who made you ruler and judge over us?"* In Acts 7: 27 Moses is confronted with the fact that growing up as a Egyptian he was not going to be accepted as leader among his own people unless he carried the trademark of Gods authority to do that. In Moses case it was not only a matter of ticking a few boxes and applying a few principles. He lacked patience, his emotional intelligence was off and he was short sighted...thinking he could free his people, one man at a time, in a 'boxing ring.'

What Moses lacked, God was ready to supply. But not instantly. Only through a process that would prepare Moses to become Gods agent for the needed transformation of Gods people. Moses fled from Pharaoh to Midian where he attended, for the lengthily time of forty years, to the sheep of his father-in-law. During the duration of this time Moses learned to develop patience with those stubborn sheep that constantly drifted away from the flock to search for greener pastures. He developed the sensitivity to know each of the sheep he was responsible for, but most of all Moses developed into a typical Hebrew who attended to the traditional nomad lifestyle that would not only prepare him for the forty years in the desert, but would restore respect for him among his own people. Having gone through this lengthily time and extended process God was ready to give him the authority to rescue his people from slavery, in a powerful revelation known to us as the encounter at the burning bush (7:30).

It is not only a matter of ticking some criteria or principles that will guarantee our congregations and our leadership to become transformational agents, but allowing the Holy Spirit the time and the process to develop us into such agents.

We see the same strategy with Joseph. Destined to become the second in charge of Egypt we are introduced to Joseph being a spoiled teenager (Gen 37:3-4). What needed to happen between Genesis chapters 37 and 41 was for God to take Joseph through a transformational process to develop him into the administrator that was needed to safe Mesopotamia from starvation.

At first Joseph was abducted and sold by his brothers as a slave to Potiphar's household an official of the Pharaoh. According to Genesis 39:2-4 Joseph was responsible to administrate and run Potiphar's household. What a great internship and training opportunity to prepare Joseph for his crucial calling. Unfortunately, with the unforeseen turn of events he ends up in gaol for an offence that he was innocent of. According to Genesis 39:21-23 Joseph was put in charge of the prison. From Gods perspective Joseph were promoted gaining more confidence as he had more logistical and administrative challenges and responsibilities to attend to. Joseph's big break came in Genesis 41 when he became Pharaoh's second in command and was given the role of Minister of social welfare (Gen 41:41-43).

CLOSING:

Satan, knowing that Jesus had not eaten in 40 days, tempts Him with food. Jesus answer's with reference to the scriptures and specifically the book of Deuteronomy. Jesus declares that during survival in the desert that our wellbeing is not depended on bread, but on God that sustain us and provide for us in the toughest of times.

Satan promises Jesus a worldly reward if he aborts His mission to die for the sins of humanity and therefore not to complete His spiritual desert in dying on the cross. Jesus replies again by using the authority of the scriptures that when journeying through ones desert it is not worldly riches and splendour that can save us (those assets is of hardly any value in a desert), but experiencing the presence of the living God.

Finally Satan challenges Jesus to proof that God and His word is reliable and trustworthy. Jesus reply can be understood as follows: He (Jesus) did not have to put God to the test for He experienced during His 40 days in the desert that God is the Protector and the Sustainer of those who put their trust in Him.

TWO GODLY PROCESSES TRANSFORMS OUR CHARACTORS TO THE LIKENING OF GOD:

- Our spiritual deserts
- The Word of God.

NOTES:

....

....

....

....

....

....

....

....

....

....

SURVIVING YOUR SPIRITUAL DESERT – SUNDAY 5

INTRODUCTION:

Matthew 3:1-12

Who would have thought that from within the Judean desert a ministry would start that would prepare a nation for the coming of the Messiah? God did not choose the Temple, the Jerusalem city centre or the Roman quarters, but He chose a barren and what seems to be an unforgiving environment to turn the hearts of the people to a righteous but gracious God. What is more striking is that the people left the hubs to enter the desert to hear John's preaching and be baptised by him. People freely chose to enter the desert if this meant that they would find forgiveness and peace. *YOUR SPIRITUAL DESERT EXPERIENCE CAN BE THE PLACE FROM WHERE GOD LANCHES A KINGDOM MINISTRY.*

CONTENT:

Why do we need more spiritual desert experiences in our lives?

- *It draws us (back) to the Messiah- Jesus Christ (Matthew 3:5-6). Repentance means to turn back....make a U-turn by turning our backs on sin and walking into the opposite direction.*

- *Our Spiritual desert is the primary place where God removes the obstacles from our lives that hinder the reception of Jesus and his Kingdom. It is the season that God strips our lives from those dead branches not producing fruit with eternal value (Matthew 5: 7-10).*

CLOSING:

The frustration that John the Baptist had with the Jewish clergy was that although they entered the physical desert to come and see what his ministry was all about they were not opening themselves up to enter a spiritual journey into the desert for that would have meant that they had to enter the hardship of being transformed by the Holy Spirit…burning up and consuming in their lives what was not of God!

NOTES:

....

....

....

....

....

....

....

....

....

....

THE SUFFERING OF CHRIST (leaves) – Matthew 27:36-56

INTRODUCTION:

Gethsemane means "Oil Press". Indicating a garden area among the olive groves on the Mount of Olives- where olive oil was prepared.

As the time was approaching fast for Jesus to face the wrath of His father, because of the sin of all mankind that he was about to take on Himself…the burden of carrying such a weight was wearing Jesus down. Jesus was overwhelmed with sorrow to the point of death in knowing that He would soon be betrayed by Judas, captured and tortured by Roman officials, deserted by His disciples, mocked by the bystanders and will eventually die among criminals. Jesus therefore spends his last evening as a free man praying with his disciples in the Garden of Gethsemane.

CONTENT:

What comes to mind when you touch the leaves?

Leaves are ***vulnerable*** *to nature. It can be destroyed in a storm and can dry out and fade in extreme heat. So too was Jesus fading in the flesh due to the knowledge that he would soon be at the mercy of the Roman authorities.*

Leaves can be easily **cut off** *from the living host plant – disconnected (Isaiah 53: 8c "For he was cut off from the land of the living.") Jesus was about to be disconnected from His own people and his disciples.*

Leaves **die!** *Jesus was the good olive that was crushed to die in the olive press. (Isaiah 53:5b "He was crushed for our iniquities").*

CLOSING:

Why would Jesus have his most intense spiritual battle in a garden? Because the biggest spiritual battle for the soul of mankind was fought in a garden (Gen 3:1-7). For Jesus to regain on our behalf what we have lost in the Garden of Eden he had to take on Satan in the garden of Gethsemane!

NOTES:

....

....

....

....

....

....

....

....

....

....

THE SUFFERING OF CHRIST (stone's) – Luke 19:28-47

INTRODUCTION:

Jerusalem was built on Abrahams mount Moriah which became later on David's mount Zion. Jerusalem became well known during the reign of King David as the capitol of the biblical nation of Israel. It became the centre of Jewish religion and worship. According to Old Testament prophecy and the Book of Revelation Jerusalem will become the City and centre of God's everlasting Kingdom. Unfortunately, we read that Jesus on His way to enter Jerusalem wept for its inhabitants...

CONTENT:

We find Jesus weeping over the 30000 inhabitants at that time as he was overlooking and approaching Jerusalem from the Mount of Olives. GOD WAS WEEPING! God in Jesus Christ was weeping over the lost opportunity. Although, so many Israelites was gathering to celebrate the Passover and preparing the sacrificial lamb as the ultimate Passover sacrifice...they did not see or seriously taken into account the words of John the Baptist who pointed to Jesus and said: This man is the Lamb of God who takes away the sin of the world (John 1:29). THEY MISSED THE OPPORTUNITY TO BE

SAVED BECAUSE THEY DID NOT UNDERSTOOD THAT THEY HAVE BEEN VISITED BY THEIR SAVIOUR AND THAT THEY WERE ABOUT TO CRUCIFY HIM.

[*Hand out a stone to each person to feel and to hold. What does it feel like? Rough around the edges? Hard and cold?*]

The reason why Jesus wept was because Israel's heart was hardened and stone cold! Looking down on Jerusalem Jesus saw religious activities (19:45-46) going on but people's hearts turned away from Him.

Like a stone it is cold…naturally the heart is as cold as ice towards the things of God.

It is hard…it cannot be cut; it cannot be broken; it cannot be moved.

Again, a stone is dead. You can find no feeling in it. Talk to it… it will shed no tears of pity.

What would it take to de-throne Satan and replace Israel hearts of stone into hearts of flesh? (Ezekiel 36:26b).

It would take God the father to turn away His heart from His only begotten Son to see the hearts of Israel turn back to Him (Ezekiel 36:26b). It was only when God turned His back on His Son to let Him die on the cross…that Israel hearts of stone would be turned into hearts of flesh! It is only through the cross that our cold egoistic hearts warm up to God. It is only through the cross that our stone cold hearts turn to flesh. It is only through the cross that our dead hearts get resuscitated back to Life.

Read Matthew 27:50-51. At that moment that Jesus died, rocks split…broke…disintegrated! What happened in the physical had a profound impact in the spiritual. I believe that the physical demolishing of the rocks that moment that Jesus died had spiritual significance….indicating that the cold, hard and dead hearts of the Jews and all mankind was finally now to come alive to God!

CLOSING:

Israel's salvation was not in its great cultural inheritance of the great City of David nor its system of religious practice. Israel were better off without Jerusalem and the temple. Israel needed the cross. It was only because of the cross that stone cold hearts turned back to God in ancient days and still does today!

NOTES:

....

....

....

....

....

....

....

....

....

....

WHY BLESS ISRAEL/THE JEWS? - SUNDAY 1

INTRODUCTION:

Romans 9:1-5/11:1-24

In Romans chapter 9:1-5 Paul explains an extreme irony. He makes the statement that the Jewish nation is the most blessed nation on earth, because God not only planned for them as a nation to receive divine blessings more so than any other nation on earth, but revealed Himself as the Messiah through Jewish ancestry! Jesus became man as a Jew to bring salvation to all mankind through Jewish culture and history. Yet, the Jews themselves did not recognise, nor accepted Jesus to be the promised Saviour of mankind.

- Paul explains that the Israelites became **God's adopted people** through whom he would introduce Jesus to the world (adoption to son-ship).
- **God revealed the divine glory of Jesus being an Immanuel God to the Jews.** In the same way that God Yahweh travelled with Israel through the desert and accompanied them in a cloud by day and in a fire by night so Jesus would journey with the Jews by becoming an Immanuel God in Jewish flesh (The incarnation of Jesus).

- **The Jewish covenants** that God agreed to with Israel was founded on Gods promises of saving Israel. Jesus became the One that fulfilled all the demands and expectations of the covenant with God so that humanity could be saved from the wrath of God.
- **The receiving of the Jewish Law** was not sufficient in saving Israel from judgement...the law revealed the necessity of a Saviour Messiah to rescue Israel from damnation.
- **The Jewish temple worship** would reveal the person and ministry of Jesus to the Jewish people as early as the days of worshipping God in the Tabernacle and Temple. Jesus would at the same time become the High Priest that served in the Holy of holies and become the slain lamb that was offered on the tabernacle and temple grounds.
- **The many promises to the Jewish people** given them by the Patriarchs and the Prophets that Jesus the Messiah would come from among them.
- **The proven Jewish ancestry that Jesus the Messiah was form the tree of David and the tree of Abraham.**

Yet in spite of all this proof did the Jews not acknowledged Jesus as the Son of God and as the saviour of the world.

CONTENT:

Because of this (the above) God set for the time being judgement on Israel:

Read Rom. 10:19....Deut.32:21

Read Rom. 10:20....Isaiah.65:1-2

Rom.11:8 which is a quote from Deuteronomy 29:4 says: "God gave them a spirit of stupor, eyes that could not see and ears that could not hear, to this very day."

This judgement simply means that in the economy of God's salvific grace he has focused his attention on the heathens and on the gentiles and blessed the early missionary outreach among these other nations (Rom.11b).

WHY THEN BLESS THE JEWS?

- This stubbornness among the Jews, made God focus his saving grace on the other nations. Because of the attitude of the Jews, **grace** was directed to the heathens and therefore is the Jews indirectly responsible for the salvation of the heathens! Rom.11:11-12. THIS IS THE GREEN LEAVES ON THE OLIVE TREE.
- Because of the Jewish Old Testament writings and teachings Western civilisation, as we have come to know and appreciate, share in the privileges of a **Judean-Christian heritage!** Christians are so to speak in grafted into the Jewish branch of ethics and moral way of life. Rom. 11:17-22. THIS IS THE BRANCHES OF THE OLIVE TREE.
- Judaism gave us **Jesus** (John 4:22)! THIS IS THE FRUIT OF THE OLIVE TREE... THAT ALL BELIEVERS SHARE IN! See Gal.3:26-29.

CLOSING:

Is God done with the Jews?

No...He never was and He never will be! Read Rom.11:1, 11 and 23, 24.

Next time we will study Gods future plans for Israel!

NOTES:

....

....

....

....

....

....

WHY BLESS THE JEWS – SUNDAY 2

INTRODUCTION:

Rom.11:25-32/Ezekiel 36:25-28/Zachariah12:10-13:1

We mentioned last Sunday that God's judgement on Israel is temporarily so that God's acts of salvation can be established among the Gentiles until that period of time is fulfil.

For this second part of the series I only need to allow Scripture to explain!

CONTEXT:

Rom.11:25-32

God can never be untrue to Himself or His promises *(Numbers 23:19).* He always keep His word to those that He has elected with the purpose of salvation. God promised the Patriarchs (The fore fathers of Judaism): Abraham, Isaac and Jacob that Israel will always be His covenant people that He will never let go of them *(Hos.11:8).* God also promised that from the lineage and family of King David and his house Israel will rule the nations. At a designated time (…until the full number of the Gentiles has come in) God will turn again his attention to the salvation of the Jewish people.

Ezekiel 36:25-28

God is like a surgeon that is preparing to do a heart transplant on Israel. This is not only relating to restoration work, but rather a complete transformation of Israel. God will take the initiative to cleanse the Jews from their past iniquities, then transform their inner personhood by giving them a new spiritual heart and mind. This will not be the work of man or the church, but supernaturally the work of God. Six times it says: I WILL.... God will by His own power and initiative save the Jewish nation and all of this will happen on a single future date *(Zachariah 3:9-10).* This will be nothing short of a supernatural miracle that can be compared to raising dead bones back to a human bodily life *(Ezekiel 37:11-14).*

Zechariah 12:10-13:1

What will the result of this transformation accomplish-this spiritual miracle? ON THAT SINGLE DAY WILL THE JEWISH NATION ACKNOWLEDGE THAT JESUS IS TRULY THE MESSIAH KING AND WILL REPENT BEFORE THE LORD! Each of the clan and families will separate themselves to humiliate themselves before Jesus!

THE JEWS WILL RECEIVE FORGIVENESS!

CLOSING:

Why bless the Jews?

The Jewish people are a constant sign and reminder to us that God can save the least among us! That if you reckon that your sin is of such a magnitude that God has rejected you...look towards the Jews and to the extent that they denied Salvation and yet God will restore them back to Him! If He will do this for the Jewish people He can do this miracle for you (2 Peter 3:9).

NOTES:

....

....

....

....

....

....

....

....

....

....

KNOW YOUR ENEMY - Genesis 2 and 3

INTRODUCTION:

The presence of the Anti-Christ has been a reality since creation. For every generation there has been occult movements and activities to try and minimise the impact of the incarnation of Jesus and the Gospel narrative.

Satan or any establishment that represents the Anti-Christ in our societies gain their strategy from a counterfeit spirit…in other words a spirit that gains its power in imitating the original. This becomes especially clear when we study the book of Revelations. In revelation we are introduced to the satanic trinity (false trinity):

- The dragon (Satan)
- The beast (Anti-Christ/the man of lawlessness)
- The false prophet (The false church)

This is a counterfeit of the Holy Trinity:

- God the Father
- God the Son
- God the Holy Spirit

This counterfeit spirit has been around since creation. It simply copies what God does and present it as the original. For example. I can print from my computer a page with a writing or a picture and then take that same page and go to the photo copier and make a precise copy of the original. Hardly no one will notice the difference. I will not only be able to confuse you in trying to establish witch paper is the original, but I can lie to you and you will not know the difference. It is this counterfeit spirit that allows for the forces of darkness to operate.

When the spirit of the Anti-Christ operates elements are not quite, as they appear to be.

CONTENT:

- **Satan makes us doubt God's good intentions for us (Gen.2: 16-17/3:1).**

  God's protection of man was established in his instruction. This counterfeit spirit now confuses to bring spiritual death to man in creating doubt.

- **Satan makes us believe that God is our opposition-not him (Gen.3:4).**

  Obedience is the factor that honours God. This counterfeit spirit now confuses in making believe that knowledge is what enlightens man. Humanity strives for more knowledge, because the more we understand, the more we can accomplish in ourselves...eventually we do not need God anymore. This spirit want to make us believe that God is keeping us from reaching such a potential.

- **Satan wants us to life in constant shame and guilt before God (Gen.3:8).**

  Shame gains its strength from sin. Satan will do everything in his power to make us to sin, because then shame and guilt can control us.

- **Satan wants us to life in constant fear of God (Gen.3:10-11).**

  When fear controls us there is not much room for the love of God! Do not confuse this with the teaching of the

Old Testament that the "fear of the Lord is the beginning of wisdom." This teaching means that to consider the holiness of God and the will of God in all our decisions and motivations will keep us from offending God and in so doing will bring blessing and peace upon us.

John 4:18 New International Version (NIV).

18 *There is no fear in love.. But perfect love drives out fear, because fear has to do with punishment. The one who fears is not made perfect in love.*

- **Satan wants us to lose faith in others and start blaming others for our circumstances (Gen3:12-13). He wants broken relationships. He wants disruption and conflict to rule our societies.**

When Eve was brought to Adam he was delighted. She was not like the animals, but someone like himself. This was the most basic entry into what we call community. When God created Eve… he established Community. In the word *community* there is some importance for us to notice: COMMON UNITY!

CLOSING:

In John chapter 14 Jesus is identified and described as the way, the TRUTH and the life. The only way to face the counterfeit spirit that the devil and anti-Christ draws on…the only way to know when you are targeted by this spirit is knowing who Jesus is in a very personal and intimate way. If you know Jesus in person…you will know the truth and that will set you free from the deceiving character of this spirit.

John 8:31- "If you hold to my teaching, you are really my disciples. Then you will know the truth and the truth will set you free."

NOTES:

....

....

....

....

....

....

....

....

....

....

KNOW YOUR PROTECTOR – Mark 5:21-34/Numbers 15:38-41

INTRODUCTION:

This Scripture describes an unusual healing. A woman who had been subject to bleeding for twelve years received a miraculous healing after she touched a corner of Jesus's garment.

Her haemorrhage did not only cause physical challenges, but social issues as well. Her condition made her ceremonial unclean to participate with others in the normal routine of religious Jewish covenant ceremonies. Therefore she was socially excluded and vulnerable. If you were impure you were not suitable to participate in the covenant and would have to remain outside of a covenant relationship with God. For any Jew to be left outside of the covenant blessing of God was more than an embarrassment, it was devastating as it effected your identity in God.

CONTENT:

The part of the garment she touched is called ציִצִת *(tzitzit)*[17] "tassels" or "fringes" worn by Jews on four-cornered garments (Num. 15:38-41). The Greek text says she touched κράσπεδον *(kraspedon)*

---

[17] Dr. Eli Lizorken-Eyzenberg.

"fringe" or "hem" and the Hebrew equivalent is כָּנָף *(kanaf)* which also means "corner" or "edge".

What many people do not realize is that כְּנָפַיִם *(kanafim)* is also a Hebrew word for "wings". Thus, in the Bible, the "corners of garments" have sometimes been compared with "bird's wings". (This is easy to demonstrate: in wearing a Jewish prayer tallit and simply walking at a fast speed you can see the edges of the tallit flapping as in flight).

What is even more amazing is that God apparently has a garment with such "corners" or "wings". The Psalmist writes, "Keep me as the apple of the eye, hide me in the (בְּצֵל כְּנָפֶיךָ) **shadow of Your wings** (Ps 17:8). "He will cover you with His pinions, and (וְתַחַת־כְּנָפָיו) **under His wings** you may seek refuge" (Ps 91:4).

This Jewish woman in the Gospels simply wanted to seek shelter in the shadow of God's wings. "But for you who fear My name, the **sun of righteousness** (שֶׁמֶשׁ צְדָקָה) will rise **with healing in its wings** (וּמַרְפֵּא בִּכְנָפֶיהָ); and you will go forth and skip about like calves from the stall" (Mal 3:20/4:2). And that is why Jesus said to her that her faith made her whole. She recognized Jesus as the Messiah and knew that as God's anointed he had God's "healing in his wings", the corners of his garment. When she reached out to touch the edge or corner of the tallit that Jesus wore she was demonstrating that she was reaching for God to shelter her.

She was testifying a wordless testimony in this demonstration: *that although religious systems may fail you (she was suspended from the covenant), although institutions like doctors and medical science may profit from you, that her only and primary hope was on the God that Jesus spoke of.* ***She was putting her faith, not religion, into action!*** *She was functioning from outside of the blessing of the covenant. Religion could not help her as she was "suspended" from the covenant. The others touched Jesus as well, but for them they were only curiously following Jesus as a religious rabbi. This woman on the other hand* touched *Jesus not to endorse her religious believes, but because she was in need of such a God that Jesus spoke of. She was reaching for deliverance, salvation… she was reaching for a saviour and redeemer, not for a theological dogma* *or new teaching of the church.* That is why Jesus said: "your faith has healed you."

CLOSING:

God is a husband to the widow. The father to the fatherless. To the injured He became the victim, the despised and the rejected:

Isaiah 53:4-5 New International Version (NIV)

4 Surely he took up our pain
and bore our suffering,
yet we considered him punished by God,
stricken by him, and afflicted.
5 But he was pierced for our transgressions,
he was crushed for our iniquities;
the punishment that brought us peace was on him,
and by his wounds we are healed.

NOTES:

....

....

....

....

....

....

....

....

....